Teaching with a Social, Emotional, and Cultural Lens

Teaching with a Social, Emotional, and Cultural Lens

A Framework for Educators and Teacher Educators

Nancy Lourié Markowitz
Suzanne M. Bouffard

HARVARD EDUCATION PRESS
Cambridge, Massachusetts

Second Printing, 2021

Paperback ISBN 978-1-68253-474-8
Library Edition ISBN 978-1-68253-475-5

Library of Congress Cataloging-in-Publication data is on file.

Published by Harvard Education Press,
an imprint of the Harvard Education Publishing Group

Harvard Education Press
8 Story Street
Cambridge, MA 02138

Cover Design: Endpaper Studio
Cover Photo: lvcandy/DigitalVision Vectors via Getty Images

The typefaces used in this book are Classica Pro, IBM Plex Sans, and Escrow Display.

CONTENTS

Appendixes

Preface

WHEN ASKED WHY they chose to work in education, most teachers talk about wanting to make a difference in children's lives. They might mention a commitment to social justice, a love of the energy young people spark, or a desire to pay forward the kind of mentoring they received when they were young. Few explain their career choices by talking about fulfilling math standards or nurturing the ability to deconstruct text. These are critical skills, of course, and teachers want their students to achieve them, but usually in service of making a difference in children's lives writ large. Most of them are focused on developing the whole child by teaching them how to persevere in their learning, build relationships, and collaborate with others—whether they put it in those terms or not. According to a national teacher survey conducted for the Collaborative for Academic, Social, and Emotional Learning, more than 77 percent of teachers believe social and emotional skills influence academics, and more than 90 percent say they have an important role to play in the classroom.[1] In another national survey, 78 percent of teachers said it is part of their job to help students develop social and emotional skills.[2]

This is not just good instinct on the part of teachers. Decades of research confirm that academic outcomes are influenced by the capacity to be calm and focused, to persevere and be resilient, to cope with stress, to navigate relationships with family and friends, and a host of other social and emotional skills.³ Living in an exciting time of epigenetic research and fMRI scans, we now have an understanding of the brain and the relationship of emotions to learning that validates what effective teachers have always known: learning is a social and emotional enterprise. Studies show that students' ability to focus, calm down, and maintain solid relationships affect their ability to learn.⁴ The practice of excellent teachers has always reflected this.

Around the turn of this millennium, however, schools started becoming inhospitable to whole-child perspectives. Amid well-intentioned efforts to raise the bar for students who have been historically underserved by schools, policies focused myopically on reading, writing, and math skills as measured by standardized multiple-choice tests, eschewing other valuable parts of education. These policies have often pushed out some of the fundamental self-management and social relationship skills—as well as the sense of wonder and curiosity—that students need to achieve and be prepared for life. It is a well-known story that need not be repeated here.

But another narrative is emerging. We have reached a point in research where educators and policymakers can no longer reasonably argue that attention to social and emotional competencies is nice but not necessary. These skills are important enough, in fact, to constitute an equity issue. Children who don't have the self-regulation skills to access instruction and do the work of learning are at a disadvantage in the classroom and beyond. Students who look or sound "different" and become alienated by derisive classmates or an unwelcoming school culture may be denied equal educational opportunities. And at a time when employers cite collaboration and adaptability among the top ten skills they look for in job candidates, to shrug off the importance of social and emotional skills is to underprepare students for economic stability and success.⁵ In fact, fewer than half of high school students in a national survey said their schools were doing even a "pretty good job" of addressing skills like working with people who are different from you, knowing how to solve disagreements constructively, and managing stress.⁶

Likewise, teachers need to come to the classroom with resilience and perseverance themselves. Those who do not are at risk for burnout and attrition, not to mention missing the opportunity to respond effectively to students and navigate student frustration, low motivation, outbursts, and other threats to academic success. This is particularly of concern in an age when nearly half of all school children have experienced at least one major adverse life event and more than 20 percent have experienced two.[7] School violence is an all too real threat, with more than one hundred people dying in school shootings in one year alone.[8] If teachers are going to respond effectively to these needs and stresses, they need to be prepared, beginning with opportunities to reflect on their own beliefs and assumptions and continuing with skill development and practice.

THE HARD QUESTION: HOW TO DEVELOP SOCIAL AND EMOTIONAL COMPETENCIES?

The hard question, therefore, is no longer *whether* schools should pay attention to social and emotional competencies, but *how to go beyond just good intentions.* Nowhere is that question more urgent than in classrooms. Principals, superintendents, and policymakers have a major stake—and a major say—in how schools approach social and emotional learning. But it is teachers who see and feel the importance of social and emotional skills every day, and teachers who have the most power to nurture those skills while students are at school. Although families will always be children's most important teachers, especially when it comes to social and emotional development, a lot of life happens during the school day—a lot of social situations that happen nowhere else, a lot of opportunities to develop one's voice, a lot of chances for a fresh perspective, and a lot of opportunities for negative messages that can hinder social and emotional development, and therefore, academic success. In short, teachers shape the development of the whole child, whether they realize it or not, and whether they are intentional about it or not.

In recent years, there has been an increasing drumbeat to make that influence more intentional and systematic. The movement is epitomized most recently, but by no means exclusively, by the Aspen National Commission on Social, Emotional, and Academic Development, a coalition of education, science, government, and private sector professionals advocating for investments in integrated approaches to developing academic, social, and emotional skills.

In our work as instructors, teacher educators, and researchers over more than two decades, we have followed this growing national and international momentum, and had some fortunate opportunities to contribute to it.

But we have not seen an adequate accompanying commitment to preparing and supporting educators to integrate social, emotional, and cultural competencies and strategies into their daily practice. Many teachers do possess these skills, but these important competencies are rarely made explicit or considered part of a coherent professional development pipeline that ensures consistently high quality from one classroom to another and one school to another. It shouldn't surprise us, then, when only about half of teachers believe they are "good at helping students develop strong social and emotional skills" and even fewer believe they have effective strategies to deploy when students don't have these skills.[9]

The fact is, when your children or grandchildren walk through the doors of school on the first day, they are entering an unacknowledged lottery. That lottery may place them in a classroom with a teacher who fosters growth mindset and encourages self-regulation skills, or in one where they will disengage after being shamed for not mastering content quickly, or left behind because the teacher believes students should sink or swim. That child's odds are further complicated by race, class, and culture; by the implicit and often unacknowledged biases all of us hold about one another; and by the impact that differences in cultural background can play in how students and teachers interpret behavior and social cues.

GOALS OF THIS BOOK: CHANGING THE ODDS

Incorporating Social, Emotional, and Cultural Competencies Throughout the Teacher Professional Development Pipeline

This book aims to change those odds. It lays out a comprehensive vision and tools for making the social, emotional, and cultural dimensions of teaching and learning a fundamental priority that can be woven into all schools and teaching preparation programs in meaningful ways, regardless of a school's resources, curricular programs, or population. It describes in detail perhaps the most powerful—but unmined—leverage point for change that exists in the field of education: attention to and development of teacher practices at each stage of the professional development pipeline, from preservice teacher coursework and fieldwork through the first two years of teaching, and continuing throughout the professional development that teachers receive in the course of their careers.

Notably, our vision does not constitute an "add-on program." We are not asking teachers or teacher educators to do *more*, and we are certainly not asking teachers "to be therapists," as we often hear educators say when we talk about social and emotional competence. Rather, the approach in this book asks teachers to work *differently*, to view students from a perspective that encourages and develops their social and emotional growth in support of academic success and in concert with the efforts of families, youth leaders, clergy people, pediatricians, neighbors, and everyone who influences the life of a child. This work is not about displacing schools' focus on math, reading, and other academic content; quite the contrary, it is about supporting it.

Build Adults' Skills in Order to Build Students' Skills

Many promising and successful efforts to develop students' social and emotional learning skills have been grounded in a framework developed by the Collaborative for Academic Social and Emotional Learning (CASEL). It consists of five social and emotional learning (SEL) competencies young people need in school and in life: self-awareness, self-management, social awareness, relationship skills, and responsible decision-making.[10] This framework incorporates both inter- and intrapersonal skills because healthy development includes components of both independence and interdependence: self-regulation (managing one's own thoughts, feelings, and behaviors in the service of goals), social awareness (the ability to take the perspective of and empathize with others), and relationship skills (the ability to establish and maintain healthy and rewarding relationships with others).[11] This five-dimension framework has been useful in driving curricular programs and goals for students, as well as some states' and districts' standards for what students should know and be able to do.[12]

But in our work with teachers, both those currently in schools and those in teacher preparation programs, we have seen an additional need for a clear set of competencies *adults* need, together with the teaching practices or "teacher moves" to help students develop SEL skills. For students to develop social and emotional competencies, adults must not only understand and value these competencies, but embody and model them. When it comes to social and emotional skills, "do as I say and not as I do" is a woefully ineffective approach. Students need their teachers (and other adults) to demonstrate the competencies and place a priority on them. A teacher who is easily and visibly frustrated by students' behavior or confusion is not well positioned to build her students' perseverance and growth mindset, for example.

Unfortunately, however, most educators receive little training in social and emotional development and how to integrate it into their practice. How to build social and emotional competencies is rarely covered in preservice teacher training programs; when it is, it is usually addressed as an isolated course with little application to practice, or as an incomplete "behavior management" approach that does not address the range of skills needed and their vital connection to culturally responsive teaching practices. A national scan of teacher preparation programs highlighted the lack of consistency in attention to the CASEL SEL competencies.[13] Nor are these skills adequately addressed in new teacher mentoring and induction programs or in ongoing professional learning for teachers and administrators.[14]

The signature contribution of this book is to link the social, emotional, and culturally responsive skills young people need with the actions that teachers, teacher educators, administrators, and policy makers can take to create environments in which these skills can develop and flourish. We introduce the idea of developing teachers' social, emotional, and cultural competencies by their use of a "lens." Much like putting on a pair of glasses helps someone see the writing in a book or the bird flying in the distance, using the social, emotional, and cultural lens moves teachers to see things, ask questions, and gather data that would be blurry or even invisible without the lens. This lens through which educators can view their practice reflects attention to key competencies, assumptions, and habits of mind of both teachers and students.

THE CATALYST FOR THIS BOOK: DEVELOPMENT OF THE ANCHOR COMPETENCIES FRAMEWORK

At the heart of the approach—and this book—is the framework developed by the Center for Reaching & Teaching the Whole Child (CRTWC): the CRTWC Anchor Competencies Framework. The Anchor Competencies Framework was developed by CRTWC over a ten-year period, beginning while CRTWC was housed at the San José State University (SJSU) Department of Teacher Education, and continuing after CRTWC became part of an independent nonprofit, as we describe in chapter 1. It was driven by data-gathering that pointed out again and again that educators knew they *wanted* to integrate social and emotional learning into their practice, but they didn't know how to do it.[15]

To respond to that gap, we began to drill down on the fundamental practices teachers need to employ in order to build students' social and emotional skills. We also recognized and honored the need to integrate culturally responsive teaching practices, which are often treated separately, but in fact are an integral part of teaching with a social and emotional lens and an integral part of effective teaching overall. We engaged in ongoing conversations and an iterative development process with teacher educators and other university faculty, preservice teacher candidates, veteran teachers and those who supervise teacher candidates, and leaders in social and emotional learning and culturally responsive teaching practices. We reviewed research as it emerged and evolved, both focused on social, emotional, and cultural competence specifically, and on effective teaching practices generally. Through this process, we developed a set of essential teaching practices that research and experience show are connected to students' success in academics, peer relationships, and ability to thrive, as well as to effective classroom learning environments that promote such success. We call these practices *anchors* to emphasize the way that they provide solid grounding for teachers' interactions with students throughout the school day and year. These practices are not separate from pedagogy in math or science; they anchor that pedagogy in the kinds of interactions and environments students need to learn everything else.

ORGANIZATION OF THIS BOOK

The book has been organized as follows: In chapter 1 we introduce the rationale behind the Anchor Competencies Framework and explain how it was developed. We describe how it can be integrated into the everyday academic learning that is the traditional focus of schools, and in a way that informs and creates coherence with other programs that are often used to address aspects of social and emotional learning, student behavior, and school climate. In chapter 2, we explain the essential elements of the framework, and in chapter 3, we illustrate how all teachers can use it in practice, regardless of the subject they teach or the context in which they work. In chapter 4, we show how the framework can be adopted by teacher training programs to get teachers started on the right foot, especially in conjunction with cooperating school districts. In chapter 5, we delve deeper into how schools can incorporate the framework as part of ongoing professional development efforts. Chapter 6 explores the ways that districts, states, and universities can help to scale this work. Finally, in chapter 7, we share a vision for the future in which all educators and students have the social, emotional, and cultural supports to thrive in teaching and learning, including the conditions needed for success and areas for future efforts.

As we describe throughout the book, the social, emotional, and cultural lens can become second nature. Teachers tell us it has not only improved their relationships with students and their students' academic and life outcomes, but has made them more satisfied in their careers and more effective and confident in their practice. It is our hope that, in reading this book and using it in your work, you will feel the same inspiration and see the same kinds of changes, whether you are a current or future teacher, teacher educator, school leader, policymaker, researcher, or one of the numerous others who are critical to students' success in school and in life. Because as one teacher put it so eloquently, social, emotional, and cultural competence isn't another thing on the plate, it *is* the plate.

CHAPTER 1

The Case for a Social, Emotional, and Cultural Lens in Teaching

IMAGINE A GORGE formed by two tall cliffs. The cliff to the left represents all of the powerful research in the neurosciences, education, and psychology about what young people need to learn and succeed. The cliff to the right represents the actual educational system. We want all teachers and children to receive the support they need, to thrive, to achieve on par with accepted standards, and to be committed to the common good. What is needed to connect the research side with the practice side so that educators traverse the gap without falling into the gorge of school failure? A sturdy bridge built with a common vision so that all the pieces fit together to create a solid, long-lasting structure.

In education, when we problem-solve about how to span the chasm, we traditionally think of programs that connect research to practice. In the case of social and emotional skills, this often takes the form of structured curricular programs that engage students in readings and activities focused on specific skills like conflict resolution or being an "upstander" who interrupts bullying. Such programs are a strong plank in the bridge we need to connect research and practice. But the struggles in schools today suggest that we need more than one plank. We need all the planks, pillars, and connecting materials in alignment. This is especially important because in the tumultuous and turnover-plagued world of schools, the program plank is often at risk of being removed because of funding changes or leadership shifts.

Now picture a sturdy bridge that you cross back and forth frequently with a clear sense of direction, confidence, and assurance of safety. It is likely made up of multiple, interrelated parts that tightly link with one another so that there are no major gaps where you could trip or fall. The Anchor Competencies Framework is like the solid concrete pilings that form the foundation for all of those parts and that ensure the bridge is structurally sound. The framework was developed to guide educators at all levels and points in the teacher development pipeline in building and holding up the bridge.

CROSSING THE GORGE: ORIGINS OF THE ANCHOR COMPETENCIES FRAMEWORK

The story of the Anchor Competencies Framework begins with the desire to cross the gorge and a lot of enthusiasm for designing something to do so ... but what? When Nancy was teaching courses on classroom management in San José State University's Department of Teacher Education, she aimed to incorporate texts and other resources that went beyond the traditional behaviorist (reward and punishment–oriented) approach in order to engage teacher candidates in learning about relationships, trust, and creating an effective learning environment for the whole child. This perspective resonated with the teacher candidates so much that they reported holding onto their course books and taking them into their future classrooms, even when they sold other textbooks back to the university bookstore. More importantly, this lens impacted candidates' interactions with students in their field experience classrooms. No longer seeing their students as challenging the teacher's authority, they stopped taking those behaviors personally. Rather, they began to delve deeper and ask different questions that led them to see these behaviors as a function of many factors, including the context that the students brought to the classroom. The longer Nancy taught the class (for more than a decade), the more it became apparent that social and emotional skills were the glue that connected everything—the relationships that teachers build with their students impacts their success at maintaining reasonable conduct expectations.

Gradually, these ideas spread among the teacher education department faculty, including a subset of faculty members who agreed to work together on ways to incorporate social and emotional skills across the program. We were supported in these efforts by the dean of the SJSU Connie L. Lurie College of Education. In the process of working together, faculty who had committed to this work asked a big and important question: What do teachers need to be able to *do* to support the development of social and emotional competencies in students? Relatedly, what do teacher educators need to do to integrate these competencies into the program's courses and field work? At the outset, it was clear that we did not have the language or adequate foundational knowledge to answer these questions.

To build that knowledge, we worked with consultants who specialized in teacher resiliency, and we continued the work of reviewing the literature on social and emotional learning. At each monthly meeting with participating SJSU faculty, we analyzed a video lesson or case study to better understand and form some agreements on what social and emotional learning looked like in practice. As we considered several possible frameworks to guide the work of integrating social and emotional learning into the program, we lit on a set of student-focused social and emotional learning competencies laid out by the Collaborative for Academic, Social, and Emotional Learning (CASEL). Because the "CASEL five" are well-recognized throughout the field and used in many schools, they provided a clear starting place. As stated in the preface, the five competencies are self-awareness, self-management, social awareness, relationship skills, and responsible decision-making. They incorporate many specific social and emotional skills detailed in the research, like emotional awareness and expression, communicating with peers and managing conflict, and maintaining focus and attention, but they are framed in easy-to-remember groups and terms.

Over the course of a year's work trying to incorporate these competencies into various teacher education classes, it became evident that faculty needed more specific guidance on what to ask teacher candidates to *do*—as well as guidance on how faculty would know if they were doing it. We knew what we wanted students to be able to do, but not how teachers could help them get there. The faculty could not yet describe what they would look for specifically in the classroom of one of their graduates that would provide them with evidence that the integration of SEL in the program was present and having the desired impact on teachers and students. Neither, it turned out, could the teachers themselves.

Through a three-year evaluation study of our initial work with faculty and teacher candidates, conducted by the nonprofit firm WestEd, we learned that graduates reported a strong commitment to bringing social and emotional competencies into their classrooms.[1] However, the graduates also indicated that they were leaving the program wanting to know more about how to actually use these skills with their students. Looking at the data, we were confident that if SJSU graduates happened to get hired into schools with evidence-based, effective curricular programs for social and emotional learning, they would be well prepared to use the programs. However, we worried that those who worked at schools without such programs would fail to integrate these vital skills in a meaningful way, and that they would be unequipped to identify or explain the social and emotional strategies they did use to others, including administrators, students, families, and teacher colleagues.

To address this concern, the Center for Reaching & Teaching the Whole Child began the process of identifying what exactly we would want to see in a classroom where social and emotional competencies were being integrated into teaching and learning—that is, what teachers could do that would translate into student skills and successes. We involved teacher educators, university supervisors, cooperating teachers, teacher candidates, and leaders in social and emotional learning in an iterative process of drilling down to arrive at a consensus of what we believed were the essential components, always firmly grounded in the research on social and emotional development and always focused on the end goal of supporting students' social, emotional, and academic development.

THE IMPERATIVE OF CULTURALLY RESPONSIVE PRACTICE

As the work developed, the faculty recognized the need for more attention to the role of race, class, and culture, thanks in part to members of the CRTWC Advisory Board, a group of educational leaders from the public and nonprofit sectors who serve as a sounding board and source of support for all of the organization's work. We had always believed that attention to culture and context would promote an equitable environment, but we became more aware of the need for the individual, family, social, political, and cultural contexts that both students and teachers bring to the classroom, as well as student learning preferences, to be front and center.[2]

We recognized the need for educators to understand that race and institutionalized racism are significant factors that influence and mediate the interactions of students and teachers from different ethnic, family, cultural, language, and social class groups. We also knew that teachers are not always able to acknowledge and act on this understanding. Teachers need extensive professional development; a one- or two-day workshop will not suffice. In an ongoing and inquiry-based approach to professional development, a safe and brave environment must be built by the facilitator with the participants.[3] There must be adequate time provided for teachers to explore their own assumptions, beliefs, and biases; how those can influence the student information they choose to look at; and how they interpret and respond to student behavior. Put succinctly by Sharroky Hollie, executive director of the Center for Culturally Responsive Teaching and Learning, culturally responsive teaching is "not something you do, but something you have in all that you do."[4]

Over the course of several years, CRTWC engaged in an iterative process of weaving together social and emotional learning with culturally responsive teaching, working with Zaretta Hammond and other experts on race and culture in schools, incorporating the feedback of teachers and teacher educators, and reading and rereading the literature by experts like Geneva Gay, Kris Gutierrez, Beverly Tatum, and Sharroky Hollie.[5] We listened to increasing criticism that the field of social and emotional learning (SEL) represents a primarily White, middle-class perspective and heard calls to connect equity issues with SEL practices.[6] This work challenged all of us in myriad ways that were essential to the work and to the evolution of the framework we were developing for teachers and teacher candidates. We knew that we needed to intentionally put context (both teacher and student) at the core of this work, and that we had to include specific examples of teacher practices that *connect* social and emotional learning with culturally responsive practices, not just put them next to each other.

THE VALUE OF THE ANCHOR COMPETENCIES FRAMEWORK

Through a multiyear iterative process, CRTWC landed on a set of seven "anchor competencies" for educators. They are grounded in and expand upon the CASEL five competencies for students but also build on decades of research about effective teaching and learning and culturally responsive practice. As such, we have intentionally linked the framework to student competencies and ultimately the student outcomes that are the goals of all of this work. The seven anchor competencies, described in detail throughout this book, are: build trusting relationships, foster self-reflection, foster growth mindset, cultivate perseverance, create community, promote collaborative learning, and respond constructively across differences. In the Anchor Competencies Framework, these seven competencies are driven by a set of specific goals, are influenced by contextual considerations, and are enacted through implementation processes, teacher moves, and specific teacher strategies. Together, these pieces of the framework serve as the roadmap to the development of a new "lens" for teaching the whole child.

We view the use of this framework as a core academic intervention that is essential to student learning and to both students' and teachers' ability to thrive. These skills and practices, situated in the individual, family, community, cultural, and sociopolitical contexts of students and their teachers, are essential to achievement, including but not limited to the attainment of standards such as the Common Core State Standards and the Next Generation Science Standards, as we will demonstrate more explicitly later in this chapter.

The framework that grew out of the anchor competencies was designed to guide teacher practice as well as student skill development; in fact, most of the competencies should ultimately be espoused by both educators and students, though the strategies to accomplish them may vary. The framework provides a common language that can be used by educators across settings, whether at a school; in a district, county, or state office; or in a university program.

FILLING IN THE GAPS

The Anchor Competencies Framework goes beyond many previous social and emotional learning approaches in some significant ways and responds to needs often voiced in the field.[7] The framework provides a more comprehensive view of social and emotional development by addressing: (1) the needs of the adults in the educational system, (2) the context of the system, and (3) the direct links between social-emotional skills, culturally responsive teaching practices, and academic skills in the full range of academic subjects.

Adults Need Skills, Too

Our approach leverages a growing body of evidence about how adults' own social and emotional skills influence students. Teachers with well-developed skills tend to develop more positive relationships with students, and research shows that those relationships are key to successful teaching.[8] The habits and behaviors that teachers model—intentionally or not—affect the habits and behaviors that students develop. In addition, teachers' own social and emotional competencies are linked with how well they cope with the stresses and frustrations of their jobs and whether they experience burnout and attrition.[9] Further, for teachers to work effectively with a diverse student population, they need to understand the students' contexts, acknowledging that they come from a range of backgrounds, including but not limited to diverse cultures, languages, ethnicities, and family structures. Teachers who are aware of and reflective about their own and their students' cultural location and social and emotional development are better prepared to model and scaffold the skills students need to succeed in school and life.

Throughout this book, we describe the importance of building and reinforcing these competencies at all levels of school systems. Just as Urie Bronfenbrenner conceptualized child development as occurring within a set of nested contexts of family, community, policy, and cultural norms, we conceptualize students' social and emotional development as occurring within a set of nested school structures and relationships (see figure 1.1).[10] Throughout this book, we emphasize not just how teachers can use the Anchor Competencies Framework with students, but how administrators, teacher coaches, and other

FIGURE 1.1   Nested school structures and relationships

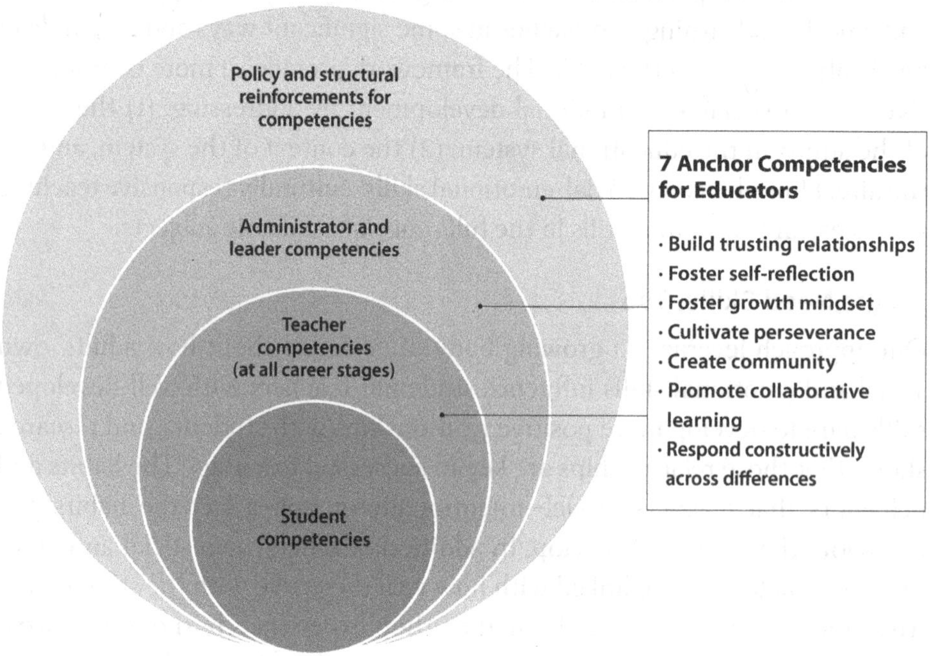

Policy and structural
reinforcements for
competencies

Administrator and
leader competencies

Teacher
competencies
(at all career stages)

Student
competencies

**7 Anchor Competencies
for Educators**

· Build trusting relationships
· Foster self-reflection
· Foster growth mindset
· Cultivate perseverance
· Create community
· Promote collaborative
  learning
· Respond constructively
  across differences

leaders can use it with teachers; how university faculty can use it with preservice teacher candidates; and how policies, like the teacher performance expectations that drive credentialing, can reinforce the competencies. After all, we cannot expect teachers to model and teach something they have not experienced themselves, and we cannot expect a safe and supportive classroom environment to blossom amid a punitive, toxic, or competitive culture among faculty or district staff. Furthermore, students are acutely aware of the adult cultures around them and, especially as they approach adolescence, they are experts at spotting hypocrisy.

Context Is Core

Social, emotional, and academic development do not occur in a vacuum. They occur within a complicated context of relationships, past experiences, and beliefs, all of which are strongly influenced by race, class, and culture. Both children and teachers live within a society of structural racism, defined by the Aspen Institute Community Roundtable for Change as "a system in which public policies, institutional practices, cultural representations, and other norms work in various, often reinforcing ways to perpetuate racial group inequity."[11] Any attention to teaching social and emotional competencies must integrate attention to the sociopolitical, cultural, community, and individual contexts that influence the thinking and actions of both adults and children.

A glaring example is the prevalence of major racial disparities in student discipline rates, which starts as early as prekindergarten.[12] The US Department of Education Civil Rights Data Collection has documented that Black students, who make up approximately 16 percent of public school enrollment, account for approximately 40 percent of suspensions nationally.[13] Studies show that Black students are more likely to be punished and punished more harshly than White students for similar behavior, and a large-scale study that compared competing explanations for these disparities suggested that 39 percent of the disparity was related to differential treatment by educators, as compared to 9 percent related to differences in behavior and 13 percent related to differential sorting of Black and White students into different schools.[14]

This disparity can be the result of teachers interpreting similar behavior differently for different groups of students. A small but telling example is Nancy's experience while working as a teacher in an inner city elementary school with a primarily Black student population. As one of the professional development opportunities provided by the district, she visited a school in a middle/upper middle–class neighborhood on the other side of town. During that visit she observed a class of fourth-grade students during transition time from writing time to math. When a few of the male students started sitting on top of their desks, letting off some steam as they changed subjects, the teacher's response was, "OK folks, clearly we need to take a little break here. Let's all take a seat in our chairs and do a few deep breaths before settling into our math work." The difference between that fourth-grade teacher's response and what Nancy often observed at her home school was striking. At her home school, teachers would have typically started taking away points from the class for the same behavior, possibly leading to reduced recess time. Teachers at her home school assumed that if they gave in to more relaxed student behavior, even a little, the whole roof might blow off their classroom management. By contrast, the fourth-grade teacher at the school she visited interpreted the same behaviors as an indication that the students needed some time and a strategy to help them settle down, so her next steps were to provide for that need, not to worry that the class was about to become unmanageable. The different teaching approaches were based on the assumptions made by teachers about their students.

The teachers in Nancy's home school conveyed a message that their students could not be trusted to manage their behavior and were not interested in learning, while teachers in the other school communicated a more positive message that their students could self-manage and were sincerely interested in learning. Such messages are often self-fulfilling predictions of future behavior.

The Anchor Competencies Framework encourages teachers to place their own and their students' social and emotional dispositions and competencies within cultural, social, political, family, and individual contexts. This prompts teachers to ask different questions, gather different data, and therefore take different courses of action based on their understanding of who their students are and what they bring to the classroom. This is one of the many things that social, emotional, and cultural competence can and should provide. In addition, approaches to social and emotional learning and culturally responsive teaching both focus on the importance of teacher empathy, reflection, and responsiveness.

Educational institutions have typically treated existing approaches to building social and emotional learning and examining issues of race, culture, and gender as separate endeavors. For example, in teacher preparation programs, courses are designated with a title to indicate the topics they are addressing, and the typically siloed courses and their titles send the message that social and emotional learning and culturally responsive teaching are independent areas of study. This is reinforced by the teacher performance expectations that state credentialing systems establish and expect the preparation programs to follow. School districts often reinforce this separation as well, by hiring separate consultants at separate times to lead professional development in social and emotional learning and culturally responsive practices, with few, if any, opportunities to connect the two. This maintains a damaging disconnect for educators and their students, suggesting different "buckets" into which they should dip, rather than facilitating an important understanding of the essential connection between them.

The Anchor Competencies Framework embeds culturally responsive teaching practices as part of social and emotional competence, and includes examples of teacher moves for helping educators make connections among the related competencies. Throughout the remainder of this book, we refer to a social, emotional, and cultural lens on teaching and learning. For ease of reading, we sometimes use a shorter version of this term, but it should be understood that social, emotional, and cultural factors are all woven together.

Social and Emotional Skills Are Academic Skills

Academic success is, of course, the goal of schools, and the building of social, emotional, and cultural competencies should be integrally connected to that goal. Some critics have understandably worried that well-intentioned efforts to promote social and emotional learning will take the focus off the core academic mission of schools.[15] But in reality, these goals are intertwined. Consider the following scenario:

> Having set a goal of improving her third-grade students' lagging writing skills, Savannah consulted the teacher's manual for the literacy curriculum program adopted by her district. Looking for ideas to support the current lesson on developing students' ability to write three complete sentences that use adjectives, she discovered that the manual recommended a partner activity. Although the manual recommended having each partner provide feedback to the other, it didn't explain the "how" of successful partner work. For example, how would Savannah make sure both students in the pair participated? How would they know how to talk with each other productively and stay on task? Savannah knew she needed to do more than tell the students who they would be partnered with, and that they should tell each other what they liked about the writing.
>
> She described her thinking process this way:
>
> "I realized that there are a lot of social, emotional, and cultural competencies that go into [effective partner work]. First of all, [students] have to have self-awareness skills to be able to explain their ideas to a partner. Then

there are social-awareness skills in terms of making sure their partner under-stands the ideas. There are relationship skills: listening to each other, hearing their partner's idea, responding, practicing active listening . . . When you are sharing your work with a peer it needs to be safe; you have to know you're not going to get laughed at and teased. The partner needs to manage themselves and their reactions, and keep it positive."

Savannah did a skillful job of making the connections between her aca-demic goals and the social and emotional skills needed to accomplish those goals. She also understood that those skills had to be taught in the same way as the academic curriculum. Had she not understood these concepts and how to infuse them into her teaching, the students might have struggled with their partners and therefore lost valuable opportunities to develop their writing and communication skills, not to mention collaboration skills.

We cannot expect students to succeed in achieving current academic stan-dards unless we are at the same time intentionally attending to the competen-cies that undergird the academic expectations. To illustrate the connection with academics, tables 1.1–1.3 present examples of standards from the Com-mon Core State Standards and Next Generation Science Standards, along with some of the social, emotional, and cultural competencies that are foundational to the achievement of these academic standards.

In the approach we propose, there is always a clear connection to aca-demic learning. For example, later in the book we describe how emotion

TABLE 1.1   Sample literacy standards from Common Core State Standards and corresponding anchor competencies

LITERACY STANDARDS	CORRESPONDING ANCHOR COMPETENCIES
Ask and answer questions to seek help, get information, ask for clarification	▪ Build trusting relationships ▪ Foster self-reflection ▪ Foster growth mindset ▪ Promote collaborative learning
Engage effectively in collaborative conversations with diverse partners	▪ Build trusting relationships ▪ Promote collaborative learning ▪ Create community ▪ Respond constructively across differences

TABLE 1.2   Sample math standards from Common Core State Standards and corresponding anchor competencies

MATHEMATICAL STANDARDS	CORRESPONDING ANCHOR COMPETENCIES
Make sense of problems and persevere in solving them	▪ Foster growth mindset ▪ Cultivate perseverance
Construct viable arguments and critique the reasoning of others	▪ Build trusting relationships ▪ Foster self-reflection ▪ Create community ▪ Promote collaborative learning

TABLE 1.3   Sample science standards from the Next Generation Science Standards and corresponding anchor competencies

SCIENCE STANDARDS	CORRESPONDING ANCHOR COMPETENCIES
Planning and carrying out investigations	▪ Foster growth mindset ▪ Cultivate perseverance
Engaging in arguments from evidence	▪ Build trusting relationships ▪ Promote collaborative learning ▪ Create community ▪ Respond constructively across differences

regulation relates to math mastery and how cultural identity shapes literacy development.

Beyond the Advisory Period

The Anchor Competencies Framework addresses how to embed social, emotional, and cultural competencies in subjects and spaces where it is not traditionally included. The benefits of connecting social, emotional, cultural, and academic development are essential, and they cannot be confined to a social and emotional learning block or weekly lesson. Yet this is still too often the way many teachers and schools have approached the skills. It is difficult to find resources that systematically look at how social and emotional learning is foundational to achievement of academic standards in each of the major content areas of literacy, math, social studies, and science. The framework allows teachers to close that gap. In a later chapter, we draw on the example of a teacher preparation program in California that has used the framework to reshape the way future math teachers think about giving student feedback, in an effort to reshape the negative perceptions many students have about the subject and their own competence.

A WORD ABOUT LANGUAGE

In this book, we have intentionally tried to avoid coining new acronyms for the work teachers do when using a social, emotional, and cultural lens. Educators are already swimming in an alphabet soup of acronyms that create confusion and sometimes cause distracting debates. Although intended to sharpen focus and specificity, a focus on terms and acronyms often leads to balkanization of efforts that actually have much in common and are best addressed together. School leaders and teachers are faced with decisions about whether to focus on preventing bullying or promoting positive youth development, on emphasizing teamwork or cultivating self-regulation. Do we not want students to be working toward all of those competencies?

That may sound like a major challenge or an undue burden on teachers. But one reason that social and emotional efforts feel overwhelming is that they have often focused on highly specific and disconnected skills, like learning to persevere or developing empathy. Each of these is important in its own right. But we have too often failed to recognize that they spring from a core set of mindsets, competencies, and strategies that live and breathe in the everyday interactions teachers have with students. Cultivating a social, emotional, and cultural lens early and throughout teachers' careers provides a through line for these efforts. In fact, the lens can be a unifying foundation for many promising efforts in schools, many of which have a long and important history, rather than work in competition with them.

BUILDING THE TEACHER PIPELINE THROUGH PROFESSIONAL DEVELOPMENT

If we really want the social, emotional, and cultural lens to be "in the drinking water," it is essential to develop teachers' skills in a coherent way, focusing

FIGURE 1.2   Teacher professional development pipeline

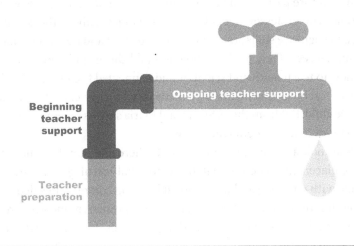

attention across the teacher pipeline through intentional professional development and support at all levels. This entails applying a common language and targeting common goals within teacher credentialing programs, within support systems for new and veteran teachers, and within programs to cultivate teacher and school leadership. Researchers and education leaders have called for attention at all of these levels.[16] But such efforts, which to date have been limited to small pockets of innovation, will be more effective if they are aligned with common goals and a common framework. The common approach represented by the Anchor Competencies Framework not only creates more continuity but can build an ongoing pipeline of highly qualified teachers who will carry this work into the core of their teaching practice and support future generations of teachers to do so as well.

Consider the case of two first-year teachers we documented as part of a formative evaluation of the San José State University teacher education program. (We have changed the teachers' names to protect their confidentiality and that of their schools.)

Susan and Maria are both new teachers, committed and passionate about social justice and equity. They attended the same university teacher education program, where professors emphasized that trusting, positive relationships with students are part of good instruction, not an add-on for those who have extra time. The professors taught teacher candidates about the social, emotional, and cognitive skills students need to succeed and how they connect to academic success. They modeled how to build those skills—even in courses about how to teach math and science—and connected the teacher candidates in student teaching placements with mentors who were experts at educating the whole child. But from there, Susan and Maria's paths diverged—and so did the outcomes of the students they taught.

Susan took a job in the same district where she had done her student teaching placement, where social and emotional learning is a district goal, complete with coaching and professional learning communities dedicated to the topic. It is only natural, therefore, that she continues to incorporate social and emotional competence in everything she does, from the warm tone of voice she uses with students, to the constructive way she gives feedback, to the way she prevents and deals with challenging behaviors.

In her first-grade classroom, students know it's ok to make mistakes, so they are willing to try anything and take the risk of sharing their thoughts. They know that their teacher won't ridicule them for a wrong answer or silly question, nor will she let classmates tease each other. They know that if they get overwhelmed with sad or angry feelings, they can calm down in the cozy "feelings corner" and then rejoin the class. As a result, her classroom is a curious, joyful, and productive place where children are constantly learning and discovering. She points out that the time on social and emotional development is well spent: "We don't have to waste time dealing with problems, and we can spend more time on instruction. It ends up saving you so much time, it's so worth it."

Maria accepted a job about ten miles away from Susan's school. Students at the school struggle with behavior problems, and her colleagues are convinced that they need to apply strict discipline. They repeatedly tell Maria that she is "too nice" and she should be more "mean" and try using sarcasm. One modeled how she mocked a student who raised her hand and said she didn't have a pencil: "Oh, no! Should I call the office?" When Maria consulted another veteran teacher about the problem of her students frequently asking to go to the restroom during lessons, the colleague told her to set a strict no-bathroom-except-during-breaks policy. "If it means they have an accident in front of their peers, that will fix the problem real quick," she told Maria.

But Maria didn't go into teaching to shame children, nor to control them. She has tried to follow her colleagues' advice to be stern, but, she says, "I can't get myself to do that. It won't come out of me even if it's in my head." She has a nagging feeling that she wants to use more of the social and emotional techniques she learned about in college, but she says that her colleagues have never even heard of the concept. And most days, she's just trying to keep her head above water. "I hate saying this, but there is so much thrown at us that it's survival mode. Last year, I thought to myself, 'I'm not using any of the things I learned in college,' and I felt kind of depressed about it. This year, my kids are so tough, I haven't even thought about it, because it's all about survival." Beset with migraines, Maria is wondering if she made the wrong career choice. And her students are way behind in the curriculum.

Susan and Maria both got a solid foundation in teacher education, and they developed similar instincts to connect with students and see their potential, thanks in part to well-trained veteran teachers who mentored them. But Maria's experience shows that what happens next in the life of a teacher matters, too. The messages new teachers receive from colleagues and supervisors have a big impact. As a result, the same teacher with the same training can walk into two different schools and come out a different educator—and her students will likely become different people, too.

We can change this. With a systemic approach and all educators working from a social, emotional, and cultural lens, teachers like Maria will be less likely to fall through the cracks—and so will their students. In addition, students will have more equitable access to the kinds of teaching and learning they need to thrive, whether or not their schools have the resources to buy a program or the good fortune to be part of a research project.

Teacher Preparation

The teacher preparation program (also called a teacher credential program) is the first and perhaps only time that teacher candidates have at least one full year to explore their beliefs and assumptions about teaching practice, their personal biases, and their beliefs about how and what children need to learn. This year lays the foundation for the rest of their teaching career. It is an invaluable opportunity to cultivate the social, emotional, and cultural lens.

(Although some teachers are trained in alternative certification programs such as residency programs or those designed for second-career teachers, approximately 80 percent of teachers are trained in traditional university teacher education programs; these programs are therefore our focus when we talk about teacher preparation in this book.[17])

Candidates take a variety of methods and foundations classes as part of their preparation, and they engage in supervised teaching practice in classrooms. There is the opportunity to provide a common thread that weaves through each of their courses and practicum placements, with veteran educators modeling what using the lens looks like in math, science, social studies, and literacy in addition to the establishment of a safe and productive learning environment. In order for this content and these experiences to happen, university teacher educators need a roadmap for what social, emotional, and cultural practices look like in a credential program. Teacher educators need to be able to state in concrete terms what they want a new teacher who graduated from their program to look like in the classroom. Further, they need to provide the candidates with a roadmap for what they will be doing the first six weeks of school—beyond what is commonly prescribed in the many "how to" books for first year teachers.

The First Years of Teaching

The preservice credential preparation will have a far greater impact if it is connected to the support teachers receive during their first two to three years of teaching. As we saw in Maria's case, all the work done in a preservice program can be undone in a teacher's first year if she does not work in a school that supports the use of the social, emotional, and cultural lens. Fortunately, many districts now engage new teachers in mentoring and induction programs, which have been found to be highly effective for both teacher retention and student learning.[18] Such programs are an ideal opportunity to help new teachers continue cultivating the social, emotional, and cultural lens. Program leaders can use the framework to identify the skills needed by new teachers and support them, with coaches continuing to provide modeling and suggested opportunities for new teachers to practice in ongoing ways.

Veteran Teachers and Teacher Leaders

As teachers become more seasoned, opportunities to continue to engage in conversations that challenge their assumptions and support exploration and testing of new social, emotional, and cultural strategies need to be available. The framework can be used in professional learning communities, coaching, teacher supervision, and leadership development opportunities that give teachers the skills to grow into coaches, curriculum chairs, or school leaders. Incorporating elements of social and emotional learning into coaching has been shown to be effective.[19] As we describe in chapter 5, Sunnyvale School District in California, which has served as a lab district for CRTWC's work on the anchor competencies, "seeds the field" with cooperating teacher and school site professional development opportunities to develop a common language and lens using the framework.

Because currently teachers vary in how much exposure they have had to a social, emotional, and cultural lens, these efforts will have to be tailored to multiple groups of teachers, including those who have been trained with the lens in mind; those who have not had any professional development in social and emotional learning and culturally responsive pedagogy, and who therefore need to be initially introduced to the lens; and those who wish to expand their capacity to include leadership work with other teachers.

In the next chapter, we describe the Anchor Competencies Framework in detail, including the intended goals, the seven social, emotional, and cultural anchor competencies that comprise the framework, and how the anchor competencies lens can guide educators to integrate these essential competencies in their work, functioning like a roadmap that teachers like Maria and Susan can apply throughout their career journeys in the hope that no one—educator or child—will become disillusioned or lost on the road to success.

CHAPTER 2

The Anchor
Competencies Framework

IN THIS CHAPTER, we dig deep into the Anchor Competencies Framework. The framework addresses both the "what" and the "how" of social, emotional, and culturally responsive teaching practice. It is intended to serve as a road-map for educators, whether they are university faculty searching for how to bring the social, emotional, and cultural lens into their methods or founda-tions courses and fieldwork experiences, or teachers in classrooms in search of how to systematically use social, emotional, and culturally responsive prac-tices to support academic instruction. When introduced to this framework, many teachers see current elements of their own practice reflected in it. They tell us that the framework gives a much needed common language for what they are doing, sometimes reinforces that what they are doing is consistent with best practices, and also opens them up to practices to which they had not been attending.

The framework intentionally covers a lot of ground, as it aims to bring together strands of research and practice that have traditionally been discon-nected. It is unlikely that all of the components will be fully digested after one read of this chapter. The goal of this chapter is to provide a full overview and a reference point, and the rest of the book reinforces specific components and their application in classrooms.

Before getting into the specific components of the framework, it's important to reiterate some foundational principles that underlie it. Social, emotional, and cultural competencies:

- Are essential to the achievement of academic standards, an equitable classroom environment, and teacher and student resilience
- Are developed in concert with and as a result of culturally responsive pedagogy, use of trauma-informed practices, and restorative practices
- Are dependent, in part, on teachers' own social, emotional, and cultural competencies
- Cannot and should not be separated from students' and teachers' sociopolitical, cultural, community, family, and individual contexts

It is also important to remember that developing a social, emotional, and cultural lens takes time and practice. It requires an iterative process of exploring assumptions, modeling, practice, and reflection. This process must be embedded throughout the teacher pipeline, starting in teacher preparation and extending through beginning teacher support and ongoing teacher professional development in order for it to become a standard part of school practices.

THE FRAMEWORK DEEP DIVE

The Anchor Competencies Framework, as shown in figure 2.1, is divided into concentric circles. This pictorial representation was suggested by Ashley Bondi, an elementary school teacher from Sunnyvale School District in California, a district with whom the Center for Reaching & Teaching the Whole Child has worked extensively, and who is a leader in incorporating the social, emotional, and cultural lens into teaching. Goals are at the center. Then, much like throwing a pebble into a pond, these goals inform what has to happen next. As use of the framework proceeds, our "pebble" leads to more and more disruption of the pond water, including changes in what needs to be included in the curriculum and how these curriculum elements are enacted.

FIGURE 2.1   CRTWC Anchor Competencies Framework

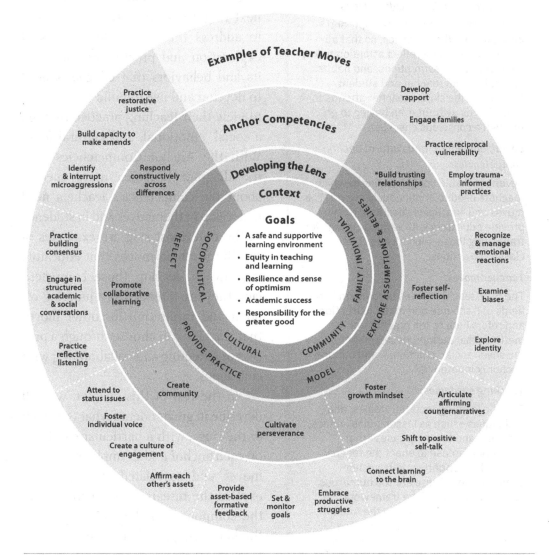

KEY DEFINITIONS

Social, emotional, and cultural lens:

A perspective that teachers apply and integrate into their practice, so that all aspects of teaching reflect attention to key competencies, assumptions, and habits of mind of both teacher and student. Eventually, the skilled teacher attends to these needs without even having to go through a conscious checklist.

Social, emotional, and cultural anchor competencies:

Seven teachable competencies to which teachers need to continuously attend. The moves and strategies described below provide educators with various options for translating these anchors into concrete classroom actions.

Teacher moves:

The term teacher moves is common in the fields of discourse and math instruction and refers here to the practices or methods that support development of the seven social, emotional, and cultural anchor competencies.

Teaching strategies:

Specific learning tools, strategies, and techniques—such as lesson plans, videos, readings, and teaching cases—that educators can use to enact the teacher moves that support various anchor competencies. These are too numerous to include as part of the framework diagram but are included in the Anchor Competencies Framework Resource Guide.[1] We provide examples of some of the strategies in this book. These strategies can help educators answer the question, "What do I do tomorrow?"

The inner circles, Goals and Context, provide direction for the work. The next ring, Developing the Lens, begins to address the "how"—the process of exploration and practice of core habits and behaviors that educators need to develop and use to build their ability to view their teaching practice through a social, emotional, and cultural lens.[2] With the Anchor Competencies ring, the diagram becomes more specific about the competencies teachers need to develop in themselves and in students. In the outermost ring are examples of specific teaching moves that educators can use to develop those competencies; they are intended as a jumping-off point and inspiration for other moves that teachers can choose through a process of reflecting and collaborating with colleagues.

In the rest of this chapter, we will describe in greater detail what is in each of the rings, with a particular emphasis on each anchor and examples of teacher moves and associated strategies. We explain the research on which each of the components is based. Throughout the book, we provide examples of how teachers can apply these anchors and use these moves at different stages of their careers.

FIGURE 2.2   Framework goals

Goals

- A safe and supportive
  learning environment
- Equity in teaching
  and learning
- Resilience and sense
  of optimism
- Academic success
- Responsibility for the
  greater good

Goals: Desired Outcomes

At the center of the framework are the intended goals of this work:

- A safe and supportive learning environment
- Equity in teaching and learning
- Resilience and sense of optimism
- Academic success
- Responsibility for the greater good

Decades of research converge on these as central goals of teaching and learning.[3] The teacher needs to provide a safe and supportive learning environment that fosters resilience and a sense of optimism in self and others. The goal of equity supports diverse students in their learning by reducing the opportunity gap so all students can achieve and thrive. The use of a social, emotional, and cultural lens supports children in achieving rigorous academic standards by building their resilience and sense of optimism, which fuels the intellectual capacity to become independent learners. Further, attention to the seven social, emotional, and cultural competencies provides ongoing opportunities for both teachers and students to develop empathy for self and others through understanding and perspective-taking that opens windows into our diverse world. The goal of taking responsibility for the greater good encourages student agency and voice to see beyond the classroom to realize and become proactive in addressing inequities in our world as teachers offer opportunities for students to engage in activities that promote social justice and support democratic institutions.

Context: Critical Considerations

If we, as educators, are to provide an equitable learning experience for all students, it is vital to understand how systems and institutions work and how they impact diverse groups differentially. The contexts in which students and teachers live affect their development, their understanding of the world, and the way they relate to each other. The interplay of cultural, sociopolitical, community, family, and individual values, policies, and practices affect everything we do, whether we are teachers, students, parents, or other stakeholders. The Context ring, by its placement in the diagram, shows that we consider it to be at the core of the work of educators, and it calls attention to the importance of these systemic factors in the successful development and use of the social, emotional, and cultural lens.

Understanding context becomes particularly important when teachers and students come from different backgrounds, have very different life experiences, or come from diverse family arrangements (foster care, adoption, same-sex marriage), as often happens in schools. For example, over 50 percent of students in US public schools are children of color, yet approximately 80 percent of the K–12 teachers who work with this diverse student population are White and female.[4] Cultural and family norms shape our behaviors, and it is important for teachers to recognize that the meaning of a student's behavior (for example, using a loud voice or maintaining a neutral facial expression even when upset) may very well be different than the teacher's own use (or lack of use) of certain behaviors. In some cultures, for instance, compliance with authority is valued over self-expression. In such cultures, the orientation toward the development of intrapersonal skills will likely be valued over the

FIGURE 2.3   Framework goals and context

development of interpersonal skills.[5] Teachers who recognize this will understand that they may need to explain why it is important for students to be able to explain their thinking, for example about how they solve math problems, and also to offer multiple ways for students to demonstrate this skill that don't necessarily involve speaking in front of the whole class or contradicting another student. The Context ring of the framework is essential to helping all of us realize our commitment to culturally responsive pedagogy and racial equity and understand what that looks like in practice.

The Social, Emotional, and Cultural Lens

Having identified the central goals and contexts, the next ring of the framework identifies the habits and behaviors that educators need to continually practice to develop and implement a social, emotional, and cultural lens in their everyday decision-making (see figure 2.4). They constitute their own ring because they apply to all the outer rings that follow; in order to develop social and emotional competencies and apply specific teaching practices to do so, teachers must continually engage in the following:

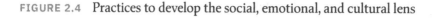

FIGURE 2.4   Practices to develop the social, emotional, and cultural lens

- Explore assumptions and beliefs
- Model
- Provide practice
- Reflect on what has happened and what to try next

These habits and behaviors are part of an iterative, rather than linear, process. They influence one another and work together. Whether a teacher is a beginner or a veteran, all four steps apply, and all take practice. Some or all of the steps may already be familiar to teachers from other aspects of teaching; if so, that should make applying them an easier process. It is important to note that they can only be implemented within a trusting learning community that encourages taking risks, making mistakes, and listening to differing points of view. Trust is fundamental to well-functioning school cultures and effective professional learning, and it must be built intentionally.[6]

Explore assumptions and beliefs

Foundational to the framework is that teachers, and those who train and support them, must critically explore their own assumptions and beliefs about intelligence, the learning process, and students. Research shows that teachers' beliefs convey messages that students internalize about the nature of learning and school, and that these messages influence achievement.[7] This should not surprise us, and it is not unique to the field of education: doctors' beliefs and assumptions, also, can affect the level and quality of care they provide to patients. Their implicit biases can sometimes lead to a lower level of healthcare for their patients of color than for their White patients.[8]

Assumptions and beliefs also impact whether teachers will value and actually implement the competencies in the outer rings of the framework or ignore them as extraneous or even inappropriate. A teacher must be willing to reflect on the meaning of culture and its influence on behavior if she is going to respond constructively across differences. She must believe that intelligence and ability can grow over time if she is going to effectively foster growth mindset.

As an example, consider Bob, who has just attended a professional development session on strategies for cooperative learning. When Bob returns to his classroom, he has not become convinced that having children work together is an important skill. But he tries the strategies because he knows his principal will be coming to his classroom for supervision and looking for those strategies. For his first group learning task, Bob decides to try a math lesson with students working on word problems in groups of four. But, not understanding the purpose and meaning of cooperative learning, nor understanding the skills needed to function well in a group, he doesn't establish routines and procedures for the group work, such as how to determine students' group roles, how to listen and be respectful to classmates, or how to make sure all group members understand the content.

Unsurprisingly, chaos ensues. Frustrated by the students' failure to work productively or to get the content, Bob decides that the students are not ready for working together and returns to his more comfortable "sage on the stage" way of teaching. Bob's assumptions and beliefs about what students need in order to learn had not been changed or even challenged. He, and most importantly his students, would have been more successful if Bob had been challenged and supported to explore his beliefs about whether group work is worth the time and effort needed to establish routines and encouraged to reflect on what his students would need from him to successfully work collaboratively.

Assumptions about race and culture are a particularly important area for all educators to explore, not just as a precursor to the other work in the framework but as an ongoing and integral part of it. We all hold beliefs about people based on race, culture, and class, and often those beliefs and assumptions are unconscious.[9] Whether from an unfair fear of someone who dresses differently from us, or an unfounded assumption about a person's studiousness based on her looks, bias affects every one of us, and we often don't realize it. Examining implicit bias is an often uncomfortable but essential part of this work.

Research suggests that teachers hold more negative perceptions of elementary school students' skills in language arts, math, science, and social studies when they are classified as English language learners (ELLs). When the researchers compared students of the same skill level who were and were not officially classified as ELLs, teacher perceptions were consistently more negative about the ELLs.[10] Yet research shows that learning more than one language is beneficial for the brain, even before children are fully proficient in both languages.[11]

Many teachers, like the one we will call Sandy, have not had the chance to learn about this research or even to think about the assumptions they apply to ELL students. Sandy sees her ELL students as deficient because they do not yet speak English fluently, rather than seeing these students as rich contributors to expanding all the students' language skills, and she believes they simply can't learn as much as other students. Consequently, these assumptions and beliefs lead Sandy to have lower expectations for the Spanish-speaking students in her class, and she ends up providing them less rigorous content and assignments and therefore fewer opportunities to succeed. Sandy is far from alone; this is common in schools and leads to a long-term pattern in which ELLs have less access to engaging and rigorous instruction and therefore to advanced coursework and college.[12] Sandy's lack of opportunity to explore her beliefs is particularly detrimental to those ELLs in her class who have already absorbed a message from society that they are incapable or less worthy of a high-quality education, including a child who has been told by strangers on the street to "go back where you came from," and another whose peers don't sit with her at lunch because they assume she doesn't know how to talk to them. For students like these, low self-efficacy can impact their ability to benefit from teachers' efforts to apply and develop anchor competencies. For example, students who do not believe they are capable will be less likely to buy into a growth mindset, and students who do not believe their teachers and peers value them will have a harder time building trusting relationships with them.

Despite its importance, exploring assumptions and beliefs is one of the most frequently missed steps in teacher education and teaching in general. When we ask about this step with teacher educators, they often respond by saying something like, "Oh, yes, we always provide an introduction to the skills for our teachers." But introducing social, emotional, and culturally responsive competencies is not the same thing as engaging educators in exploring their personal assumptions and beliefs around those skills and what it takes to develop them. This exploration can influence teachers' understanding of the skills and how well they ultimately develop and apply them.

Model

Teachers tend to teach the way they were taught.[13] That is true of both preK–12 teachers and university teacher educators, and it is highly limiting, given all the advances in our knowledge of best practices over the past few decades. To address this, teachers and teachers in training need opportunities to see other examples that are grounded in research and best practice, and to reflect on them and how they might differ from what the teacher or candidate is currently doing. Many schools and districts use coaching, an effective form of professional development in which veteran teachers model best practices and guide teachers to incorporate these practices.[14] In teacher education, this kind of modeling can be provided by ensuring that teacher candidates learn in practice, not just in theory. For example, a study of New York City teachers found that teacher preparation that focuses more on the work of the classroom and engages participants in the actual practices involved in teaching, such as planning guided reading lessons, produces teachers who are more effective during their first year of teaching.[15] These findings suggest that teacher preparation programs should consider increasing the integration between methods courses and practice in the field.[16]

We believe it is important for modeling to start with teachers and teacher educators exploring their assumptions and beliefs about what constitutes good teaching and how to get there. From there, they are well positioned to incorporate what they see and hear from good modeling. Modeling includes providing multiple examples of effective teaching with a social, emotional, and cultural lens across the curriculum and throughout the classroom day. We have watched how classroom teachers and teacher candidates, when provided multiple opportunities to watch excellent modeling enacted by teacher coaches, site administrators, in video lessons, or when given opportunities to read case studies of practice and analyze them together in a learning community, gradually understand what the social, emotional, and cultural lens in teaching looks like in practice. In teacher preparation, candidates will benefit from multiple opportunities to see modeling of best practices using the lens across their coursework and in their field assignments. This means, of course, that the cooperating teachers with whom candidates are placed in the field must have their own understanding of and ability to use the lens. Because we have found that to be a gap, we have provided training to cooperating teachers as well as teacher candidates.

Provide practice and reflection

Practice in teaching to the competencies and then reflecting on what happened—what worked, and what did not, and what one should do next time—is essential to teachers' evolving skill development. This is an iterative process, and one that is similar to the tenets of improvement science, a research method that tests short cycles of practices or interventions and makes modifications before continued testing.[17] When talking about this process of refinement, we use the word "practice" even for veteran teachers and those who have been using the lens for many years because, like the practice of medicine or architecture, the skills of great teaching should always be improving over time.

For example, at one week's session in her classroom management course, Nancy encouraged candidates to practice one mindfulness activity in their field placement. The next week, she asked the candidates to reflect on what had happened. One of the candidates, Max, indicated that the exercise had not gone well—several of his sixth-grade students had started giggling, and few had actually engaged in the activity. His initial thought was that he just could not do this kind of exercise with his students. However, some of his classmates then shared what had happened in their classes. Leslie shared that she did some preparation with the students before starting the activity, talking about how they might feel uncomfortable and that was okay. John shared that he had first talked about some of the research on mindfulness with his students, and how it helped the brain do a better job of concentrating. Both Leslie and John indicated that it had not gone totally well for them the first time they tried it, but that by doing it each day, the students were starting to appreciate it and actually remind them to do it! Max, hearing about the experiences of his peers and having the opportunity to reflect on what he might do to increase success in using mindfulness practices in his classroom, decided to go back the next day and try again. And the next week, he came in to share that students were starting to respond positively.

The ongoing practice of exploring assumptions and beliefs, observing powerful modeling, practicing strategies in the classroom, and reflecting and learning from what happens so as to continue improving is described in many of the examples we share and in our recommendations and advice throughout this book. In all of our work, we encourage educators to remember that developing a social, emotional, and cultural lens is never "done" and that no one fully masters it. Rather, all of us (including Nancy and Suzanne) continue to sharpen the lens over time.

The Social, Emotional, and Cultural Anchor Competencies and Teacher Moves

The third and fourth rings of the framework (see figure 2.5) identify the "what" and the "how"—the competencies that educators need to work on with students and within themselves, and examples of how teachers can put them into practice. The anchor competencies are the skills, knowledge, and habits that contribute toward the central goals of this framework—they are the meat of the work. They are what make educators effective at cultivating social,

FIGURE 2.5   The seven anchor competencies and teacher moves

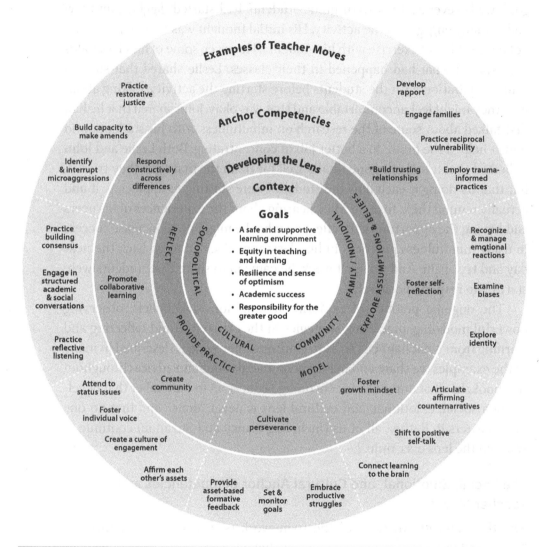

emotional, and cultural competence, and are therefore the essential ingredient to improving students' outcomes.

None of the seven anchors can stand alone and several may be present or overlap in a given class period, content lesson, coaching session, or professional learning community meeting. We put an asterisk next to Build Trusting Relationships, because we think of it as the "super anchor" that needs to be present in order to address any of the other anchors. That said, each anchor requires attention to the others to achieve our goal of developing individuals and a society where children and adults are able to flourish, achieve their potential, support one another, and contribute to the betterment of the world. There is no one right anchor to begin with. All are important and should ultimately be addressed, but where teachers begin is dependent on their students, classroom needs, and school context.

The seven anchors are:

- Build trusting relationships
- Foster self-reflection
- Foster growth mindset
- Cultivate perseverance
- Create community
- Promote collaborative learning
- Respond constructively across differences

These anchor competencies were derived through a process of reviewing a variety of SEL frameworks and, as mentioned earlier, work with diversity consultants.[18] To ensure that we were staying grounded in the needs of the field, CRTWC also created a group composed of university teacher education faculty, university supervisors, school administrators, and cooperating teachers to provide feedback each step of the way.

In articulating the anchor competencies, CRTWC recognized that we needed to explain what the anchors look like in practice, that is, what behaviors teachers perform or use. To flesh this out, we were inspired by the literature on high-leverage teaching practices developed by Deborah Ball and her colleagues at the University of Michigan.[19] The idea of identifying key practices related to the social, emotional, and cultural lens, just as Ball and her colleagues had done related to general teaching practice, made sense. But we also recognized that there are nearly limitless ways for teachers to enact the anchor competencies, so any specific practices we included would be examples rather than a definitive list. This approach also matched our goal of wanting teachers to internalize and then apply the anchor competencies, not employ cookie-cutter activities or a checklist of approaches without reflection. To be clear that these examples are meant to be flexible and inspire other approaches, we called them *moves*, a term that a math educator at San José State University suggested based on his background in the use of "teacher moves" in math education.[20] We liked the term because *move* connotes fluidity, individualization, and a personal style. Think of a dance move, a chess move, or a tactical move. They are not selected, multiple-choice style, from a predetermined checklist. But you can recognize them, replicate them, and learn them; in fact, people who are learning to dance, play chess, or develop strategy often do learn from lists of moves others have used before them. This helps a novice (or even a veteran) understand and get comfortable with the underlying skills and then apply them in ways that work for them.

The moves help further define what these anchors intend to address and, in particular, deepen understanding of how each anchor draws from both social and emotional learning and culturally responsive teaching. The examples of teacher moves are also intended to promote further understanding of how many of the areas being given attention in teacher practice, such as trauma-informed teaching, growth mindset, and social justice, can actually be thought of as under one umbrella rather than kept in separate buckets of study and practice. In past efforts, some of these approaches have been employed as stand-alone strategies, sometimes billed as magical pills to solve schools' problems—promises that, unsurprisingly, they aren't able to fulfill. Our goal is to show how these pieces can fit together as part of an overarching social, emotional, and cultural lens on teaching and learning.

Anchor One: Build trusting relationships

Decades of research show that positive, supportive relationships between teachers and students are important for student success.[21] Perhaps this is best expressed in the familiar adage, "People don't care what you know until they know that you care." New teachers have access to a wealth of books on how to lay the foundation for positive learning environments in their classrooms, and in most of them, building relationships with students is one of the first things mentioned.[22] While this might seem an obvious strategy for educators to pursue, we cannot make the leap that all educators view building trusting relationships with students as key to student learning and development. Consider high school teachers who work with up to 150 students each day and often perceive their job as instilling content and skills in their students. They may see building trusting relationships as "nice but not necessary" and not foundational to their work.

Using the teacher moves of developing rapport with students, engaging families, practicing reciprocal vulnerability, and employing trauma-informed practices are essential if a trusting relationship is to be built between student and teacher.[23] Understanding the importance of issues of attachment in relationship building is equally critical.[24] Students need to believe that both the teacher and their peers "have their back" if they are to take the risks required to succeed academically. Teachers may find that other moves are also beneficial; those listed here are merely a starting point and a set of ideas for building relationships.

Building a trusting relationship requires more than caring about students, and more than just asking how students are feeling when they come to school in the morning or what they did over the weekend. Underlying the work of building routines with students, encouraging kindness in teacher/student and student/student interactions, and fostering care about one's work is the need for the teacher to think intentionally about the context that their students and they, themselves, bring to school.[25] This includes paying attention to the individual and family situations that can significantly impact students' and teachers' daily lives as well as the racialized society in which we and our students live and learn.

It is important to remember that teachers' relationship-building strategies are essential to work with all the other anchor competencies. Teachers continually model for students the way we expect them to treat one another and care for one another, including how they treat others who are different from them. As with all of the anchor competencies, building relationships is a skill that is equally important for educators and their students to develop.

Anchor Two: Foster self-reflection

Self-reflection is a simple way to dig deeper into your feelings and find out why you were doing something or feeling a certain way. Teachers who engage in self-reflection can think about what is working and what is not working in content teaching, and whether their responses to students help the students move forward in their understanding of the academic content, their understanding of themselves, and their interactions with their peers.[26] Similarly, students who self-reflect on their learning and their learning processes can assess what they have and have not mastered and self-direct their efforts. They can also apply the skills of metacognition to adjust their approaches and learn how to learn better.[27]

Teachers who promote reflective classrooms ensure that students are fully engaged in the process of making meaning. They organize instruction so that students are producers, not just consumers, of knowledge. The teacher helps the students monitor their own progress, construct meaning from the content learned and from the process of learning it, and apply new learnings to other contexts and settings.[28]

For example, one teacher used Lev Vygotsky's "zone of proximal development" theory to teach her high school students to self-reflect on how hard particular assignments were for them. She started by introducing Vygotsky's

FIGURE 2.6   Adaptation of Vygotsky's zone of proximal development

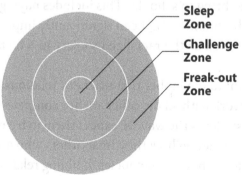

theory at the beginning of the year with the figure 2.6 diagram (which she adapted for the purpose of engaging modern-day adolescents).[29]

The "challenge zone" is akin to Vygotsky's concept of the zone of proximal development—the ideal space for learning, in which students are challenged beyond what they can do independently, but just enough that they can master new learning with the help of an adult or a more experienced peer. The students used a paper version of this diagram to indicate the level of difficulty they experienced when doing an assignment, and they shared this self-reflection with their teacher. This exercise, conducted periodically over the entire year, helped students assess how challenged they were by particular activities and also helped them generate strategies to deal with being in the "freak-out zone" or the "sleep zone." This is a great example of how to apply the anchor competency of self-reflection with students.

Given our goal of bringing social and emotional learning and culturally responsive teaching practices together, we note the importance of recognizing and managing one's emotions as part of self-reflection, through such strategies as mindfulness practices.[30] In addition, we include a focus on the hard work of examining one's own biases and exploring one's identity as one source of emotional responses.[31] While examining internal biases can be very difficult, not doing so will lead to a deepening of the status quo in how we respond to students.[32] This, in turn, will limit the teacher's ability to establish the trusting relationships needed if students are to overcome individual, community, and societal obstacles to achievement. Both teachers and students, by engaging in self-reflection about their work and their relationships to others, are increasing their ability to self-regulate.[33] Further, they are expanding their repertoire of responses when they feel stressed, when they have difficulties with others, and when the work at school becomes challenging.

Anchor Three: Foster growth mindset
This anchor refers to the development of both the students' and teachers' beliefs that they can learn more and become smarter if they work hard, seeing mistakes as furthering their learning rather than showing their lack of competence. People with a fixed mindset believe their basic qualities, like their intelligence or talent, are simply fixed traits and that talent rather than effort

creates success.[34] The child with a fixed mindset may believe that she is not good at math and therefore, she will never be good at math. The teacher candidate with a fixed mindset, after conducting a lesson that completely unraveled, may believe that he is just not meant to be a teacher. In both cases, rather than believe that they just haven't acquired certain skills yet, they believe they cannot do it. A fixed mindset among students leads to stress as they believe that nothing they do will help them get better in a particular academic or social-emotional area.

People with a growth mindset believe they can always learn more and improve. Students who embrace growth mindsets will view challenges and failures as opportunities to improve their learning. It's important to note, especially when working with students, that growth mindset is not just about telling students to try harder and persevere. It has become common to focus primarily on helping students assume the stance that if they try hard enough to learn something, they will get it. But a growth mindset isn't just about effort. Students need to try new strategies and seek input from others when they're stuck. They need this repertoire of approaches—not just sheer effort—to learn and improve.[35] The misguided "just try harder" efforts often fail to take into account the context that students bring to school, including the messages they hear at home, in the community, and in society at large. Those messages can be detrimental, whether they are about girls having lower ability in math and science than boys, or about African American students being less likely to succeed in college. The teacher needs to understand the narratives or beliefs that students have about themselves that may arise from dominant societal narratives and be able to articulate affirming counternarratives that provide students with a different and more positive internal message and shift their internal voice to positive self-talk. With this revised internal narrative, students are much more likely to persevere with difficult tasks.

For example, it is very likely that immigrant students, particularly if they speak Spanish as their first language, are affected by the current societal discussions and climate that are anti-immigrant. If they buy into these societal stereotypes, they are likely to need someone who has status to disrupt those stereotypes. The most likely person who can do so is their teacher. The teacher has the ability to both gradually uncover the dominant narratives the students are carrying and then to articulate counternarratives that affirm the students' worth. Further, teachers can provide students with examples of positive self-talk that actively move them beyond the tapes they are carrying in their heads.

Anchor Four: Cultivate perseverance

Perseverance is continuing to try and working toward a goal even when it becomes difficult or frustrating. We want to encourage and develop students' ability to stay with a task, project, or long-term learning goal to help them understand new content or develop new skills.[36]

Perseverance is clearly connected to other anchor competencies, especially growth mindset. If you have a growth mindset, you will likely see the importance and benefit of persisting toward your goal. If you have a fixed mindset, you are likely to believe there is no reason to try. Fostering self-reflection by attending to the student's zone of proximal development will help encourage persistence. While "grit," or stick-to-it-iveness in the face of difficulty has been talked about at length, we find that other concepts and frameworks do more to acknowledge the role of context in shaping perseverent habits, and they have more potential for intentionally helping students to develop these skills and attitudes over time.[37] In fact, one review of the literature suggested that "the primary utility of the grit construct may lie in the perseverance facet."[38]

Teachers can encourage perseverance by believing in each child's ability to achieve, giving positive feedback, and helping students realize that everyone makes mistakes. What is most important is the message that they should keep trying, and that mistakes are part of the learning process and should be celebrated, not hidden.[39] It's important to teach children how to regroup and start over and to encourage them to take responsibility for themselves and make constructive choices. Teachers can help cultivate perseverance by the messages they send, the kind of feedback they provide, and the kind of tasks they present, engaging students in productive struggles that challenge them, setting and monitoring goals, and encouraging students to learn from their mistakes and keep trying.[40] For example, Suzanne once heard an elementary school principal say that she realized she needed to change her message to students before the state standardized test, from saying "Good luck" to "Do your best and draw on what you know."

Anchor Five: Create community

This anchor focuses attention on building a classroom where students feel like they belong, and where they feel connected to one another and to their teachers. Sadly, a 2006 national study on school climate found that only 29 percent of sixth through twelfth graders found their schools to be caring and encouraging places.[41] This is striking given that research has found that a positive school climate improves academic achievement and reduces the negative effects of poverty on achievement, boosting grades, test scores, and student engagement.[42] Indeed, new knowledge about human learning and development demonstrates that a positive school environment is not a "frill" to be attended to after academics and discipline are taken care of. Instead, it is the primary pathway to effective learning.[43]

To build this kind of classroom the teacher needs to apply a variety of moves. One such move is fostering individual voice, which refers to respecting and honoring the values, opinions, beliefs, perspectives, and cultural backgrounds of individual students and groups of students in a school. To do that, teachers' instructional practices should incorporate students' interests and passions, and, when possible, allow students some choice in learning activities.[44] Another valuable strategy is creating rituals and routines that create both predictability and students taking responsibility for their classroom and its community. Suzanne saw one teacher do this by creating a "fun box." When students did something kind, helpful, or challenging, the teacher asked the student to choose a card from the fun box, all of which involved engaging the class in a celebration like a dance move or turning to the person next to you for a high five. As with all of the anchors, this kind of strategy on its own doesn't build social, emotional, and cultural competence, but it is one of many kinds of activities that can build a positive community that lays the foundation for other skills and development.

Another part of building community is ensuring that all students feel a sense of belonging.[45] For that to happen, teachers must attend to the way that students treat each other as well as to status issues among students, because students who feel put down by others, or who perceive themselves to be of less value or popularity, will not feel part of the community. Teacher feedback can address student status issues in the classroom.[46] The teacher has the power and authority to provide specific feedback that identifies and reframes students as skillful in particular areas, particularly those who otherwise may be marginalized, for whatever reason, by their peers.[47] For example, in one fourth-grade classroom Nancy observed a teacher ask the students to solve a math word problem in groups of four. As she went around the room, listening in on the dynamics and content of their group talk, she stopped at one table where two boys and one girl were going back and forth with each other on what they thought they should do. The fourth boy, a Chinese American student named Max, who tended to be quiet and who spoke limited English, was working on the problem by himself using the Unifix cubes the teacher had provided. The teacher came over to the group, noted out loud that Max was doing a great job of problem-solving using the cubes, and suggested that the other group members could ask him what he was doing. Here, the teacher was giving the student status with the other students, by showing them what he had to contribute and that she valued him as a member of the classroom community.

The teacher must also work to create a culture of engagement, in which students feel connected to what they are learning and are motivated to do the work and engage in the thinking that leads to learning. Engagement is often conceptualized along three dimensions: *cognitive* engagement, thinking about the task at hand; *behavioral* engagement, action related to the task; and *affective* engagement, feeling connected to the task.[48] To establish a culture where students feel engaged, the teacher should start with positive relationships (the super anchor), because they have been shown to foster the three dimensions of engagement.[49] But engagement is about more than relationships. It also comes from conducting learning activities that are interesting and relevant to students' lives and backgrounds. For example, Suzanne saw an example on social media of one teacher who made a poster that said "How LeBron are you feeling today?" with pictures of the basketball star—universally beloved by her students—in nine different emotional states, to connect her work with the students on emotional awareness to something relatable and important to them. And culturally responsive teaching experts point to the value of using music and dance to encourage attention to emotions, community, and social connectedness among students.[50]

It's important to remember that the culture of community extends beyond the classroom. Teachers can facilitate student engagement in service learning projects and encourage them to work toward social justice within their community. Teacher moves that promote the importance of giving back to your community can help students embrace a sense of responsibility for the greater good and for helping to create a place where all affirm each other's assets. Again, these are moves consistent with culturally responsive teaching practices and the attention to communalism that is foundational to these practices.[51] If student voice is valued, and if the teacher explicitly and continuously addresses status issues that arise in the classroom, students are likely to feel like they belong and therefore want to participate. Feeling like they are part of a large classroom family, students are more likely to persevere.

Anchor Six: Promote collaborative learning
Collaborative learning refers to instructional strategies that require students to work together toward a collective goal as well as demonstrate individual accountability.[52] (It is also sometimes referred to as cooperative learning.) Students are actively working with their peers on skills development and content in a meaningful way. This focus on group interdependence, harmony, and collaboratively working toward a goal, can help students of all cultures learn, and it is a starting point for building a shared classroom culture.[53] This kind of shared thinking and learning is associated with higher achievement and more positive attitudes about school.[54]

Key teacher moves include: practice consensus building, engage in structured academic and social conversations, and practice reflective listening. The ability to form, express, and exchange ideas is best taught through dialogue, questioning, and the sharing of ideas. Specific strategies include "think-pair-share" and socratic seminars, but there are numerous ways to promote peer learning. Collaborative learning strategies can be used by teachers to structure opportunities for students to practice engaging in focused academic and social conversations and learn how to listen and respond, particularly when there are disagreements. Rich academic conversations promoted by collaboratively structured learning opportunities can lead to, among other things, increased literacy skills, empathy, engagement, motivation, and equity in student experiences.[55]

Anchor Seven: Respond constructively across differences
In today's world, differences abound. The complexity of these differences—whether they be racial, gender, linguistic, or cultural—can be overwhelming for the classroom teacher, especially when opinions and potentially hurtful comments can be shared more easily and quickly—and even anonymously—than ever before because of social media. And these differences cannot be dismissed as only occurring in certain neighborhoods or geographic areas within the United States where there are traditionally high numbers of immigrants, refugees, or people from a certain cultural background. Some of the states with the highest proportion of English learners, for example, are Alaska and New Jersey.[56] But respecting and responding constructively to differences is about far more than race and language. Students who are homeless, living in foster care, adopted, physically disabled, navigating mental health problems, or who depart from the so-called "norm" in myriad other ways are present in all of our classrooms. And too often, these differences lead to or exacerbate conflicts among students or even between educators and students or their families.

In order for teachers to prevent and respond effectively to conflicts that arise across differences, they cannot be asked to take on the role of therapist nor can they turn a blind eye to all of these differences. They can and should be provided opportunities to self-reflect on internal biases that may influence their own expectations of students, and therefore build their capacity to build trusting relationships with all their students and engage in practices that reflect the belief that all of their students are capable, both academically and socially.[57]

Teachers must also believe that students can be taught to respond productively to the diversity within their classrooms and school, and they must engage the students in learning why and how to do so. This means that we need to focus on teaching students rather than on punishing them. In schools, educators often deal with conflicts through "behavior management" approaches. As evident by its name, however, behavior management sees the teacher as controlling student behavior rather than teaching them to reflect on it and change it. This perspective has led us to reward those who behave as they are told, and punish those who do not. However, brain studies now can show us that punitive responses activate a fight/freeze/flight brain response, shutting down access to self-reflection and other forms of executive function.[58] In this fight/freeze/flight state, it is not a matter of the student not wanting to respond, it is that physiologically, they cannot respond using their prefrontal cortex. The teacher moves of building student capacity to make amends, giving them strategies for responding and acting differently, interrupting microaggressions, and practicing restorative justice build student and teacher capacity not only to work effectively across differences but to actually use those differences to build a more caring world where diversity is valued.[59]

PUTTING THE ANCHORS TOGETHER

It bears repeating that no anchor competency can or should stand alone. For example, we would not expect to see a teacher lead a community-building activity without also expecting that the teacher had been extensively engaged in building trusting relationships, fostering self-reflection, and practicing collaborative learning skills. Furthermore, these anchors are applied in the context of academic instruction. If we aren't applying the lens to the curriculum, what would students be reflective *about* and what would they cooperate *on?* It is *during* their learning about math, social studies, and other content areas that these skills must be developed and applied.

For example, consider that one of the expectations included in current academic standards is the ability to explain one's position on an issue or answer to a problem, not only in writing but also in front of peers. This is no easy task. It takes courage to speak up. How many of us have been in group settings as adults where we have hesitated to ask a question or make a comment for fear of being seen by others in the group as lacking in knowledge? Children in a classroom can see themselves as equally at risk, perhaps even more so because of the power dynamics and the authority adults hold, for example, over whether students will be promoted to the next grade or get to participate in a special enrichment program. Furthermore, the fear of being bullied is real; a child might fear being mocked because they don't know the answer, or speak with an accent, or, conversely, for being a show-off or "acting White" if they *do* know the answer.[60] Clearly, we want to create an environment in which students are willing to take a risk and speak up, leading to greater learning. To do so, educators need to address multiple anchor competencies:

- *Build trusting relationships* between teacher and student, and among students, so the students feel safe enough to speak without being ridiculed.
- *Create classroom community* where students feel like they belong and are supported by their classmates whether or not they make a mistake.
- *Foster growth mindset* so that students recognize they will become more knowledgeable if they put themselves out there.
- *Cultivate perseverance* to make it easier for students to speak up, ask questions, and try again and again because they are in a classroom environment that explicitly encourages and reinforces that behavior.

There are countless situations like this that arise in the daily lives of students and teachers. As the anchor competencies and teacher moves get "in the drinking water" of schools and become second nature for teachers, the more opportunities teachers and students will have to benefit from them so they can thrive academically, socially, and beyond. In the next chapter, we illustrate what that looks like and how educators can use the framework in concrete ways.

CHAPTER 3

Integrating the Framework in Classroom Practice

TO BE SUCCESSFUL, the Anchor Competencies Framework needs to live and breathe in the culture of schools, including in schools' discipline policies, learning groups, daily interactions between educators and students, and among educators in the school. When the framework is successful in classrooms, teachers weave the anchor competencies into their everyday practice, not just during a forty-minute lesson once or twice a week. This means paying attention to the messages they send about the value of effort and cooperation, managing their own emotional reactions to students, and engaging students in conversations and activities that reinforce the anchor competencies.

This is illustrated nicely by the teaching practices of Rachel, a first-grade teacher who is also a cooperating teacher for a teacher candidate. As part of her professional development as a cooperating teacher, Rachel learned to incorporate the seven social, emotional, and cultural anchor competencies into her teaching. That prepared her well for the following scenario, which CRTWC staff had the opportunity to observe and film one spring morning, when the class had benefited from nearly a full year of social, emotional, and culturally informed teaching.

As a new week began, Rachel was excited to begin teaching her students about haiku poetry. When the morning bell rang, she stood by the classroom door to welcome her students, as she did every day. She greeted each student by name and instructed the group to put away their things and form a circle on the rug. But she noticed immediately that Juan was upset—he looked like he had been crying, he shuffled his feet, and dropped his backpack on the floor in front of his cubby. Rachel approached Juan, kneeled down to be eye level with him, and softly and discreetly asked him to share how he was doing. Juan explained that he really missed his mom. Rachel knew that his parents were divorced, and when he spent weekends with his father, he was sad not to have time with her.

Rachel recognized that given the level of Juan's sadness, he might spend the entire morning thinking about how he missed his mom rather than about class instruction. So before she headed to the rug to lead morning meeting and introduce haikus, she quietly suggested to Juan that he make a card for his mom telling her how much he missed her. He would be able to give her the card when she picked him up from school.

As Rachel began the class's morning rituals, Juan sat down at his desk, took out a piece of paper, and began to draw. About ten minutes later, he quietly walked over to the rug with the other students and took a seat. Within a few minutes, he was fully engaged and participating in the discussion with the other children. He even got excited to write his own haiku.

Rachel was using the competencies outlined in the Anchor Competencies Framework. She welcomed each individual into the classroom as a strategy to build a trusting relationship with her students and as a way to gather data on their mindsets and readiness to learn that morning. Seeing Juan clearly struggling with his emotions, she focused him on doing something constructive with his feelings, lowering the stress hormones that flow through the brain and body during negative emotional times and giving him a chance to express his feelings and then move on from his tough morning. Not only did this help Juan in the moment to reengage in the classroom, but Rachel fostered self-reflection, enabling him to practice recognizing and managing his emotional reactions. This took little time or effort, and no money. Most importantly, it took no focus away from instruction of the class; in fact, it increased Juan's focus on instruction.

Beyond attending to an anxious child's emotional state, Rachel built the competencies into the routines and daily habits of her class. Before beginning the lesson on haiku, she did a quick check-in with her students to assess everyone's emotional state and promote everyone's mindset for a productive lesson, which she did with them on a regular basis. First, Rachel took the "temperature" of the class by asking the children to indicate, with a hand signal, how they were doing that morning. Did they feel raring to go? That meant give a thumbs-up. Did they feel a little off, maybe because they didn't get enough sleep that night because their sibling woke them up? Thumb to the side. Or did they have a rough morning, maybe because of an argument on the way to school, or because mom or dad was stressed about paying bills? Thumbs-down.

In about one minute, Rachel was able to gauge how each of her students was feeling, which she knew was going to influence the extent to which they would be able to engage in the lesson. As part of her ongoing work of building trusting relationships, she also indicated how she was feeling (thumbs-up) to engage in reciprocal vulnerability. She showed that she was ready, along with the other children who had indicated thumbs-up, to be a support to those students who were struggling more that morning. Here she was acknowledging that not everyone is going to feel great all the time, and that is okay because they are a caring classroom community where they can count on others to support them when they need help.

At the same time, she wanted to give students the opportunity to refocus and put their tough mornings behind them, if necessary, or to simply clear their minds for the academic work to come.[1] The next step she took before starting the lesson was to do a short mindfulness activity, a calming, centering activity that took only a few minutes. Mindfulness is best cultivated as an ongoing habit, and Rachel had been working on this all year with her students, introducing them to different techniques and getting them in the routine of using them.[2]

In fact, Rachel saw mindfulness exercises as being so helpful in focusing and calming both her and her students during the school day that she decided to develop a sequence that she and other teachers could use to bring mindfulness into the classroom (see sidebar).

On this day, she called upon a little girl in the class to choose and lead one of the mindfulness activities. The student chose a breathing in and out exercise

MINDFULNESS CLASSROOM IMPLEMENTATION

Rachel Bacosa

Supports self-management, self-awareness, fosters self-reflection

BUILDING THE 1ST LAYER OF MINDFULNESS

Discussion of what it is, how we use it, and what it could look like.

- Provide language and vocabulary about mindfulness. Mindfulness means paying attention to what is happening right now. Mindfulness does not mean sitting and not doing anything.
- Why do we do it in class? It helps us to pay attention, to calm down when we are upset, to make good choices, and to regulate our emotions.
- When is it a good time to do it? When you are losing your focus, feeling unsure, worried, tired, angry, stressed, and need a break.
- What do our bodies and mouths look like when we do it? Our bodies are still and quiet. Our mouths are relaxed and being used to breathe in and out.
- What can our partner/community expect from us? Our partner/community can expect that we do this together. To set up everyone for mindful success, we will be respectful with our bodies and honor each other's mindful space.

BUILDING THE 2ND LAYER OF MINDFULNESS

- Practice the foundational skills
- Practice mindful body vs. unmindful body (mindfulschools.org)
- Practice mindful listening with chime/bell/singing bowl (mindfulschools.org)
- Practice mindful senses discovery (use a sense and an object or nature)
- Practice mindful walking

BUILDING THE 3RD LAYER OF MINDFULNESS

- Practice everyday mindfulness
- Morning routine/morning circle (on the carpet, same time, same format, provide a poster of choices and refer to it)
- During content blocks—every 20–30 minutes
- Before, during, and after tests
- After transition times
- After recess/after lunch
- After a pull out (such as gym, music, or library)
- While walking to a pull out (do mindful walking)
- To read the pulse of your class
- To read your own personal pulse

called Starfish Breathing (wakeupschools.org/starfish-practice-getting-in-touch-with-your-breath/). After the two-minute activity, Rachel again checked in with the class, asking them to indicate, by showing their thumbs again, how they were feeling about getting to work now. Many more thumbs went up. Rachel had paid attention to how the students' individual life contexts and current moods would influence their readiness to learn, and she was working on the anchor competency of fostering self-reflection in the process.

CONNECTING THE ANCHOR COMPETENCIES WITH ACADEMICS

It is clear from the examples above that incorporating the anchor competencies can both help students get ready to learn and keep them intellectually engaged. But they can also support specific academic standards. Here's what happened the following week in Rachel's classroom:

In keeping with the California standards for literacy, Rachel spent a week introducing a literacy unit on writing haiku poetry. With a classroom that looked like the United Nations due to its great diversity, it was important to her to represent cultural diversity in the books she used. She had previously gathered together a menu of culturally diverse books that all related to haikus and that represented the cultural and racial identities of her students. She had been sharing these books with her students at story time each day. On the day we filmed, she used *Basho and the Fox*, a fable about a seventeenth-century haiku poet in Japan whose poems are rejected by a sly fox, as the impetus for the students to begin writing their own haiku poems.[3] In this story the poet is initially confident that he can meet the fox's challenge of writing a "good" haiku so that the fox will let the poet eat the delicious cherries from a nearby tree. However, he finds his confidence severely challenged as the fox rejects one haiku after another. But the poet's perseverance and resilience lead to his eventual success.

As she planned the lesson, as shown in table 3.1, Rachel thought about both the academic skills she was teaching and the anchor competencies she needed to address for her first graders to be able to do this rigorous work. The academic standards she intended to teach that day included the following (from the California Common Core State Standards for English Language Arts & Literacy in History/Social Studies, Science, and Technical Subjects):[4]

- Describe characters, settings, and major events in a story, using key details.
- Identify words and phrases in stories or poems that suggest feelings or appeal to the senses.
- With prompting and support, read prose and poetry of appropriate complexity for first grade.
- Demonstrate command of the conventions of standard English grammar and usage when writing or speaking.
- Use frequently occurring adjectives.
- Participate in collaborative conversations with diverse partners about grade 1 topics and texts with peers and adults in small and larger groups.
- Follow agreed-upon rules for discussions (e.g., listening to others with care, speaking one at a time about the topics and texts under discussion).

As any teacher knows, this is quite a long and complex list! Rachel believed that in order for her students to succeed in this rigorous work, she was going to need to weave social, emotional, and cultural competencies throughout. So, as part of her lesson planning, she explicitly identified the anchors that would provide foundational support to achieve the academic learning objectives she was going to address. Her plan was to work on the anchor competencies by asking questions that required the students to first analyze the behavior of the character (third-person analysis), and then draw connections to themselves.

After reading the book, and as she got ready to lead the discussion, Rachel set the stage and created a trusting and safe environment by sharing a story of her own, an example of a time when she hurt a friend's feelings because she canceled a lunch date with that person. She talked about how hurt her friend was and how she had to put herself in her friend's shoes to understand why she would be so upset. Once she did that, she came up with a strategy to make amends with her friend by apologizing and setting another date. By sharing her own feelings about a difficult situation with a friend, Rachel created an environment where the students felt able to talk about their own hurt feelings. In this example, Rachel was building trusting relationships with her students by exhibiting the teacher move of reciprocal vulnerability.

TABLE 3.1   Haiku lesson: Basho and the Fox

ANCHOR COMPETENCY	TEACHER MOVE	DISCUSSION PROMPTS
Build trusting relationships	Reciprocal vulnerability	▪ Teacher shares her story of problem with a friend. Asks students what problems they have had with friends.
Foster self-reflection	Recognize and manage emotions	▪ How is Basho feeling throughout the story? How do you know? Can you name the emotion he has? ▪ How can you relate? Have you ever felt rejected after working hard at something? ▪ How does Basho manage his emotions? Think about the strategies we used in our class to manage our emotions.
Cultivate perseverance	Use the character in the story to model what perseverance looks like, and then have students identify how they practice perseverance	▪ How does Basho persevere throughout the story? What are some examples? ▪ How do you persevere when something is difficult for you?
Foster growth mindset	Encourage positive self-talk by providing model of character in story	▪ What does Basho do to bounce back from disappointment?
Build trusting relationships	Use character's actions to model skills in building relationships	▪ How does Basho respond when the other characters initially disappoint him?

Developing the Social, Emotional, and Cultural Lens

Rachel planned questions for the story of Basho that gave students the opportunity to think about their assumptions regarding why characters made particular choices in the ways that they interacted with one another. She then talked about actions the characters and the children could take. After referring to the example of the canceled lunch date with her friend, Rachel gave the students the opportunity to practice responding constructively across differences, by asking them if they had ever been upset about something they had done to a friend or family member, and if they had then thought about it and taken some action to make amends. Because Rachel had first modeled doing this herself (using the teacher move of reciprocal vulnerability), several students readily shared instances where they had been mad at someone, like a sibling, but then thought about the other person's point of view and made amends. As a result of this modeling and practice, the students engaged in a lively discussion about the behavior and decision-making of the characters throughout the story.

The complexity of teaching is very apparent here—in the process of engaging the students in what was a very animated discussion, Rachel was both using appropriate anchor competencies and addressing the following academic standards from the list above:

- Describe characters, settings, and major events in a story, using key details.
- Identify words and phrases in stories or poems that suggest feelings or appeal to the senses.
- With prompting and support, read prose and poetry of appropriate complexity for first grade.
- Participate in collaborative conversations with diverse partners about grade 1 topics and texts with peers and adults in small and larger groups.
- Follow agreed-upon rules for discussions (e.g., listening to others with care, speaking one at a time about the topics and texts under discussion).

The discussion then led to small group work where Rachel asked the students to consider what details they wanted to include in their haikus to describe their own characters' personalities, behaviors, and actions. In this part of the lesson, Rachel was teaching to these academic standards:

- Demonstrate command of the conventions of standard English grammar and usage when writing or speaking.
- Use frequently occurring adjectives.
- Participate in collaborative conversations with diverse partners about grade 1 topics and texts with peers and adults in small and larger groups.

THE FIRST STEP TO APPLYING THE ANCHOR COMPETENCIES: BEGINNING THE SCHOOL YEAR

Although the anchor competencies can be developed at any time, in our experience it is easier and more powerful to begin working on them at the very beginning of the school year in order to build a solid base of relationships, create a safe environment for learning, and set the tone and expectations for the students. As most teachers will attest, what happens in the first few weeks of the school year establishes patterns that tend to persist, for better or for worse. As a result, we often hear new and soon-to-be teachers ask, "What do I need to be doing the first weeks of school to lay the foundation of a strong and positive classroom?" The anchor competencies provide a helpful way to answer that question and get teachers off to a good start by creating an environment that is safe, supportive, and equitable, encouraging student resilience, optimism, academic success, and a sense of responsibility for the common good. In the following section are some of the ways we have seen teachers use the anchors to set the right tone for their classrooms at the beginning of the year.

Build Trusting Relationships

To begin, the teacher needs to focus on creating a safe and supportive learning environment by building trusting relationships with her students and among the students themselves. Many strategies and activities can be used to do this.

One beneficial strategy is welcoming each child individually into the classroom each morning, paying attention to their affect as they say good morning, and exchanging a few words with each child about their weekend, or an exciting classroom activity coming up, or a child's pet. (It can be helpful for teachers to let parents know that this is an important part of their morning routine with children, which helps them gather data about how everyone is doing and how ready they are to learn. The teacher would therefore let the parents or caregivers know that she prefers to set up other times to talk with them about concerns or questions they have, so that the morning focus can be on the students.)

The teacher might begin another routine of bringing the students together for a morning meeting and using various techniques to gather information about what is going on in their heads as they begin the school day.[5] (The thumbs-up activity Rachel used is just one of many check-in activities.) We all have our "on" and "off" days for a variety of reasons—our children are sick, or we had a misunderstanding with someone. Children are no different. A teacher who tunes in to her students' emotional states is going to use the time that she welcomes each of them into the classroom to assess their emotional state for the day. She is going to be able to respond to a child who looks distressed in a positive, supportive way before that child either disengages for the day or perhaps acts out.

Another activity we have seen teachers use in the beginning of the year, especially in the early elementary grades, is reading stories about life transitions and differences among people. A teacher might read a book about a child's first day of school in a new context, such as Yangsook Choi's *The Name Jar,* about a child who does not yet speak English.[6] This book normalizes the nervousness students usually experience when they start a new school year in a new class (whether or not they are English learners), and provides a springboard for conversations about welcoming everyone into the classroom, including those who are different from ourselves.

These conversations are especially important in classrooms where students (one or many) come from diverse cultures or speak languages other than English. The teacher might plan some lessons using pieces of literature such as Jacqueline Woodson's *The Day You Begin* or Alexandra Penfold and Suzanne Kaufman's book, *All Are Welcome*, to initiate a discussion about how it feels to be different when you go into a new place, and to open a conversation about what students and other people in the students' community or country think about immigrants and English learners.[7] Such lessons give the teacher the opportunity to provide a counternarrative to racial and ethnic stereotypes by emphasizing how great language learning is and how students can honor and support it in their classroom. Through these conversations, the teacher can raise the status of the English language learners by asking students to discuss the advantages of having classmates who speak more than one language. The teacher can make the discussion proactive by leading the class in discussing what kinds of strategies they will use to help their classmates who are learning English or who have recently moved from another country.

Another option for building trusting relationships is engaging in reciprocal vulnerability. For example, if the teacher has herself lived in a place where she did not speak the language, she can share her feelings of frustration, concern, and perhaps sadness in not understanding what those around her were saying. Then she might ask if anyone in the class has ever felt that way for any reason and is willing to share. If the students start sharing their feelings in what they perceive as a safe setting, they begin to build trusting relationships through engaging in reciprocal vulnerability. The teacher is helping them lower their stress and therefore increasing their ability to concentrate and learn.

These kinds of conversations and activities don't take a lot of time and, in our experience, they pay off quickly and for the long run in students' outcomes, including their social and emotional skills, their cultural competence, and their ability to focus on and master academic content. Yet they are not covered in many of the plethora of books available about the first weeks of school and about classroom management. The Anchor Competencies Framework therefore fills an important void.

Foster Self-Reflection

Fostering self-reflection is an ongoing habit that all of us—whether students or adults—have to work on over time. But a common and powerful practice to establish this habit at the beginning of the year is to create a routine of using mindfulness practices. Mindfulness activities, like the breathing activity Rachel's students engaged in, have been shown to help students calm themselves and become more focused.[8] They can be helpful for everyone, but particularly for students who may be suffering from trauma or anxiety—or just having a difficult day. Many wonderful books have been written and videos produced with specific examples of how to begin mindfulness activities in the classroom and use them effectively throughout the school day and year. Using such tools, the teacher may start a routine of doing a mindfulness activity every morning, or even a few times during the day, as needed. Teachers should first lead and model mindfulness strategies with the students, but it helps students take agency and develop self-regulation for the teacher to gradually transition to asking for student volunteers to lead the mindfulness exercise, as Rachel did with her first-grade class. When we observed that class, it was palpable how much the energy level had calmed down among the group of students after the exercise.

Teachers can also establish the habit of self-reflection at the very beginning of the year through the kinds of questions they ask and the feedback they give about student work. For example, they can model explaining how they came up with an answer to a math problem, or ask a student to explain his thinking about the motivation of a character in a book. The teacher can let students know about—and then follow through with—a plan to ask them to review their work and the comments on it, and to discuss where they made mistakes, why, and how they can correct them in the future.

Foster a Growth Mindset

During the first weeks of school, the teacher can also begin fostering a growth mindset. She can introduce the students to what it means to have a growth mindset by talking to them about the growth process involved in learning and by reading books like *Your Fantastic Elastic Brain*.[9] Although it can be helpful to hang posters with phrases that remind students about the power of a growth mindset, it is even more important to embody those messages in the way one talks to students, sets them up for tasks, and reacts when they complete tasks. Giving students multiple chances to demonstrate their competence—rather than just one test—can also help reinforce this message.

It is also helpful for teachers to study and be responsive to the way children see and feel about themselves as students, including their self-efficacy. By asking students to complete a survey or having some discussions with them about their favorite subjects, the subjects they have trouble with, and the kind of friend they think they are, for example, the teacher begins to get a sense of the internal narratives that dominate their thinking and may make it hard for them to approach certain situations or subjects with a growth mindset. This can help the teacher begin strategizing to provide alternative, more productive counternarratives. For example, it is unfortunately very common for students to believe they were just not born good at math and science.[10] A teacher who identifies this at the beginning of the year can immediately begin to provide the students with counternarratives to what they may have heard and internalized outside of school. The teacher can also create and reinforce a message early and often that students are stretching their "math muscles" when they encounter a problem they don't know how to solve.

Through strategies like these, the teacher is also addressing the anchor competency of fostering self-reflection by using the teacher move of examining biases that may be informing students' willingness to persevere, as well as their reactions to various curricula and to one another.

Cultivate Perseverance

Cultivating perseverance is something that teachers must do in their ongoing interactions with children—by encouraging them to keep going when they get stuck on a math problem, giving them more than one chance to complete a difficult task successfully, and emphasizing the role of mistakes in learning. But teachers can lay the groundwork for this anchor competency by discussing it with students at the beginning of the year. They can give students multiple chances to try an assignment or activity, and encourage their effort rather than the outcome. Teachers should also model perseverance by playing a game or trying an activity at which they do not immediately succeed and at which they have to persevere, being careful not to show frustration but instead to voice their thoughts about what they are trying and learning.

Teachers should also make it clear that a community of learners succeeds or struggles together, and that the class will work together and support one another until everyone succeeds. In the very beginning of the year, teachers can help encourage this by, for example, playing cooperative games, either board games or physical education games. Students often quickly begin to support one another and send messages such as, "If you keep trying, you'll get it," and, "We will help each other."

Create Community

Community building should start from day one, because social patterns and classroom climates become established quickly, and it's important that the climate be a positive and supportive one, in which students learn and progress together. One beginning of the year activity that can be used from upper elementary all the way through high school is a snowball activity. First the teacher asks the students to write on a small piece of paper what makes them feel safe in a classroom and what they worry about in a classroom. Then the students gather into a large circle, crumple up their pieces of paper, and put them in the big hat that the teacher takes around the room. The teacher then empties the contents of the hat in the middle of the circle. One by one, the students randomly select a piece of paper and read it aloud. As the students read, the teacher lists on the board or a large piece of paper what the students have said they want for a safe classroom. This list forms the basis for a discussion of class norms and for a class-generated list of expectations and agreements.

The teacher can also begin a yearlong practice of acknowledging publicly and positively the strengths and gifts each person brings to the class, from knowing another language, to offering kind words when classmates are down, to knowing how to draw animals or play musical instruments. The teacher should also intentionally use classroom activities so that everyone can show and be acknowledged for their own talents, and so that they get in the habit of learning those things about each other.

Even simple getting-to-know-you activities can help foster community right at the beginning of the year, even when students don't know each other well. For example, some classrooms use the "ball greeting," where each student takes a turn calling out a name and tossing the ball to that classmate, and each day or week the class is challenged to improve how quickly they can complete the naming task and work together to make sure everyone gets the ball.

Promote Collaborative Learning

Collaborative learning is closely connected to classroom community, because it is difficult, if not impossible, to have real collaboration without trust and mutual concern. In addition to the community-building and relationship-building activities already described, the teacher can begin to cultivate collaborative learning by having students work together toward a mutual goal from the very beginning of the year. For example, by providing pairs of students a task, perhaps putting together a puzzle or a treasure hunt in the early grades, or solving a logic puzzle in the upper grades, teachers begin to show that in this classroom, everyone supports one another and that working together will lead to a better outcome than doing it alone. It helps to foster self-reflection about collaboration at the conclusion of this activity, such as by having students discuss what they contributed to their shared goal and what they learned from one another. It's also valuable for teachers to begin establishing routines and skills for cooperative learning structures in order to scaffold the skills and steps they need to make those partnerships succeed.

Respond Constructively Across Differences

Undoubtedly, conflicts will arise among students—they are human after all! These can happen for all kinds of reasons, even among students who do not have behavior problems and who have relatively strong social and emotional skills—for example when one student gets frustrated, another feels left out, and yet another impatiently wants to move on. Using the social, emotional, and cultural lens, the teacher sees these emotional reactions as normal and as an opportunity for growth and learning, rather than an indication that the students are difficult or that they are not ready to work together. It's important for the teacher to help students learn to work to respond constructively across differences, and to start the year off by letting students know that all during the year, they will use these "glitchy" moments to brainstorm alternative ways to respond. For example, if students forget to respond to one another in a caring and supportive manner, instead of threatening to keep them in at recess, the teacher might call the class to a meeting on the carpet. She might then help them think through how they were treating their classmates and ask them for suggestions to make amends and to behave differently in the future. At the end, they would be asked to actually make amends for the situation that had occurred.

For example, consider the interaction between a teacher named Mark and some of his fourth-grade students during a math lesson on place value the first month of school. A group of eight students, together with Mark, were sitting in a circle on the floor. Mark asked them to look at the number 1440, which he had written on a little whiteboard, and discuss with a partner the difference between the two 4s. After a minute of partner discussion, he asked Jose to share what his partner had said. His answer was not correct, and Andre, seated on the other side of the circle, piped up with, "No, you're wrong." In a very neutral tone, Mark asked Andre to think about how he might have said that differently. He shrugged his shoulders, essentially saying "I don't know," so Mark suggested two alternative responses which he also wrote on chart paper so they would be able to refer to these in the future: "I disagree" and "You don't have it yet, but let me show you how I figured it out." Mark then moved on to the next number for them to discuss. There were no behavior cards turned, points lost, names put on the board, or shaming of Andre in any other way. Instead, Mark used the interaction as a teaching moment, setting the stage and providing feedback on appropriate responses during group work. By the spring of the school year, when slipups inevitably occurred, he would be able to refer students to the chart, which would by then have multiple suggestions for supportive responses, which they would practice using.

Misunderstandings and misperceptions are particularly likely to occur when people don't know each other well, which often happens at the beginning of a school year. It is important for teachers to acknowledge at the beginning of the year that we are all different in many ways and that is something to be celebrated. She can start by asking students to share something that makes them unique, like the story behind their name, or unique qualities or talents they have, and what they hope to learn about each other during the year. In the process they will also find out qualities and interests that they have in common! But teachers should keep in mind not to put students on the spot or force them to talk about the things that make them feel different, nor should they be the ones to call out what makes one student different from another. This is never a good idea, but can be especially detrimental in the beginning of the year when there is not yet a trusting, supportive community in place.

A COUNTER EXAMPLE: THE STORY OF MOISES AND A MATH LESSON GONE AWRY

Sometimes the social, emotional, and cultural anchors are most conspicuous by their absence. To demonstrate, we sometimes use the following example in our work with university faculty and teacher candidates.

In 2009, Richard Levien, an independent filmmaker, created a twelve-minute film called "Immersion" about an English learner student and his teacher (available at www.immersionfilm.com). The film prompts participants to take a look at a well-intentioned but underequipped first-year teacher, Rebecca, who misses the chance to support an English language learner, Moises, who clearly excels in math. His family, while not formally educated past the sixth grade, strongly supports his getting a good education. At one point in the film, Moises is in his fifth-grade class, and the teacher is giving the students the following word problem:

> A boy ran three blocks in six minutes. If he continued to run at the same speed, how long did it take him to run the next twenty blocks?
>
>   A. 30 minutes
>   B. 18 minutes
>   C. 40 minutes
>   D. 1 hour

The teacher then asks students to raise their hands if they think they know the answer. Three students raise their hands, but all are clearly guessing. In the meantime, Moises has been making sense out of the problem on his paper and comes up with an answer. Julio, seated just behind Moises, looks over on Moises' paper, sees the answer, and raises his hand. The teacher calls on Julio and he provides the correct answer: 40 minutes. However, the teacher then asks Julio how he got the answer and, of course, he can't respond, so he says he just forgot. Moises then timidly raises his hand. The teacher, excited to see him trying to participate, calls on him. Amazingly, he gives the correct answer as well! The teacher gets even more enthusiastic seeing him provide the correct answer. So she asks him to explain how he got his answer. However, he speaks and understands very little English, so he responds by repeating the answer. The teacher tries to gently coax a response out of him two or three times. He keeps repeating the answer but nothing else, since he doesn't understand her question, posed in English. The other students start lightly giggling, but gradually they begin to laugh. The teacher reprimands the class, indicating that if they don't stop laughing they may lose their recess break. Moises is left feeling embarrassed, and the other students are blaming him for their getting reprimanded. The teacher is feeling frustrated. The lesson clearly did not go as planned.

What went wrong in that lesson? There appeared to be little if any content learning, and even more significantly, students did not demonstrate any social, emotional, and cultural competencies. It is important to note that the teacher cared about Moises and all the other students and wished the best for them, but her good intentions were not enough to prevent the disappointing outcome of the lesson. Unpacking this lesson using the Anchor Competencies

Framework demonstrates how using the social, emotional, and cultural lens can help teachers analyze what has happened in a lesson that will ultimately further their teaching competence and therefore student learning.

First, there appears to be no evidence of a trusting relationship or community among the students, given the students' lack of support for Moises and their willingness to have a bit of fun at his expense. The students do not feel comfortable saying they do not understand how to do the problem—rather, Julio chooses to say he "forgot" how he got the answer. Moises surely did not feel like his classmates "had his back" as he tried to give his answer. Students had not learned to be patient with one another. They were making fun of Moises' inability to understand and speak English well enough to fully participate.

The fact that Julio was looking on Moises' paper for the answer would suggest that these children did not value perseverance over a quick possible right answer—whether they understood the answer or not. Were the students encouraged to embrace productive struggles or self-reflection, Julio might not have seen the need to look over at Moises' paper, and he might have understood the inappropriateness of giving the teacher Moises' answer without giving him the credit.

Further, the teacher fell back on the traditional way to respond to the situation; that is, in her effort to encourage Moises to share his thinking, she inadvertently put him on the spot by asking him to explain, in English, how he solved the problem. She also was jeopardizing any community she had tried to build with the students—she threatened the class with punishment when they started laughing at him, and Moises became the student who got the others in trouble. As Moises struggled to understand what the teacher was asking him to do, class management was falling apart, he was feeling frustrated, and no doubt, the teacher was not feeling very good either.

What's important to note here is that this situation resulted in more than embarrassment and hurt feelings. It resulted in a lost learning opportunity for Moises (and for Julio, who never had to understand where the answer came from), and it likely made Moises even more reluctant to speak up in the future with questions about content or ideas on which the teacher could elaborate. It may have even made him doubt his ability, which could, in the long term, result in decreased effort and motivation.

To further emphasize how critical the anchor competencies are to academic achievement, we can also analyze this scenario in terms of English Language Development Standards, such as those used in California:[11]

- Exchanging information and ideas with oral communication and conversations
- Offering opinions and negotiating with or persuading others

Did Moises feel safe enough to try to explain his thinking or, put another way, "exchange ideas with oral communication"? The answer is no. Was he in a position to "persuade others" of the correctness of his response? Again, the answer is no. The lack of trusting relationships and classroom community inhibited the ability of the students to take risks, to learn new skills, and to engage effectively with one another. He did not have high status as a student, and the teacher was unable to provide him that status—which he needed if he were going to be able to offer opinions and persuade others without fear of being ridiculed.

Might anything have gone differently in the above scenario if this teacher had been prepared in a teacher preparation program where she had learned about the Anchor Competencies Framework, understood the anchors, and had the opportunity to practice using them in the classroom? How would that knowledge, and practice in implementation, potentially have impacted what happened during that lesson? Instead of a frustrating experience for both teacher and students, with no learning occurring, could it have been a lesson that left students excited about new mathematical understandings? Put more simply, if the teacher had put on her social, emotional, and cultural lens glasses, what would she have done differently?

The math class scenario could have ended differently for Moises. He wanted to share his idea for the correct answer, and he wanted to be able to do it orally—but he was not quite ready to do so in English. Nor did he understand enough English to know what the teacher was asking him to do. We will now "rewind" the lesson showing how it could have ended quite differently had she started the year by laying down the seven anchor competencies. If it had looked like the following scenario, which Nancy created for teacher educators during a Teacher Educator Institute session, this lesson could have become a great opportunity to practice those anchors within the context of the math curriculum.

Rebecca shows a problem about time and speed on the board. She then asks the students to think about how they feel about diving into the problem by showing their right thumb—up if they are ready to try; to the side, if they are not sure and feel a little concerned; and down, if they do not understand it at all and feel like they would like to just forget about it. Most of the children put their thumbs down—it is new content and Rebecca knows it is going to be challenging. She tells them she can totally understand those who are really concerned about it, while also acknowledging those who are feeling ready to start. She tells the students that when she saw the problem in the book she initially became very tense and concerned about how to solve the problem (reciprocal vulnerability). But she also tells them that she reminded herself to take some deep breaths to calm herself down so her brain could work better (shift to positive self-talk). She reminds them that they all need to have the dopamine rather than the cortisol flowing into their brains (connect learning to the brain). She then puts them in groups of four, with at least one person who is strong in math in each group. This was a collaborative learning skill they had acquired over the course of the year. Rebecca gives them the following directions: they need to discuss the problem, decide on ways the problem can be solved, and be sure that everyone in their group can explain their thinking and suggestions. Since the students had also learned from the beginning of the school year about what it means to be an English language learner, how great it is to be bilingual, and how to support their peers in the classroom who did not speak English as their first language, they view their peers who speak a first language other than English positively (affirm each other's assets). So they have strategies to support them when they are in their groups. The students go into their groups, come up with some strategies to solve the problem, and make sure that everyone in the group can explain the strategies they generated. The teacher then calls time and asks one group at a time to go up to the board to share their strategies. Since they had learned from the beginning of the school year that making mistakes is essential to learning (growth mindset), they are not fearful of being laughed at by the rest of the class. After each group shares their ideas, the teacher helps them look at all the strategies and decide which one(s) would work. The recess bell rings but two of the groups, including the one Moises participated in, ask to remain in the classroom so they can try out the strategy and see if it actually works! After recess, Moises, together with his group, shares his answer.

In this alternate version, Rebecca didn't have to work more or harder, just differently. That is the power of the social, emotional, and cultural anchor competencies. It is important to note that what happened in the video could have occurred even in a class where the teacher is mindful of attending to social, emotional, and cultural competencies. A key difference is that we would expect a teacher who teaches to the anchors to see the episode as a learning opportunity rather than a disciplinary issue. If Rebecca had been working on the anchors all year, she might have brought the students together in a class meeting to reflect on what had just happened. She might have exhibited reciprocal vulnerability by starting the conversation with acknowledging that she had put Moises on the spot. She could have then asked the students what they might have done differently to support Moises.

HOW WILL WE KNOW IF THE ANCHOR COMPETENCIES ARE IN PLACE?

Even among educators who believe in the importance of social, emotional, and cultural competence, it can be difficult to know whether the anchor competencies are in place. Can administrators or coaches walk into a classroom and identify specifically the practices the teacher is using that foster these competencies? Can university teacher educators walk into the classroom of one of their graduates and assess whether they are using what they have learned about integrating the competencies into their teaching practice? Often, the answer to these questions is no. To change that, educators need specific guidance about what to look for, and tools for observing and reflecting on whether and how classrooms employ appropriate social, emotional, and culturally responsive strategies—not lessons—and create environments conducive to learning for all students. The Center for Reaching & Teaching the Whole Child developed some tools and techniques to help educators and leaders at all levels implement the framework and recognize the competencies when they see them.

Lesson Plan Template

In schools across the country, and in teacher preparation programs that ultimately influence how students are taught in those schools, a common process is lesson planning, and a common tool is the lesson plan template. Lesson plan templates help guide teachers' thought processes. Writing a detailed lesson plan is particularly helpful to candidates, as it provides practice in rigorously thinking about instructional decisions.[12] Following the prompts on a template, the teachers typically need to think through the entire lesson, from what materials will be needed, to how the students will be grouped, to the lesson objective, steps for reaching the objective, and how they will assess whether they succeeded. Lesson plan templates—which look different from place to place—provide a good opportunity to make sure the anchor competencies are applied and to create cohesiveness around the Anchor Competencies Framework, whether in elementary or secondary classrooms or across teacher preparation programs in which teacher candidates are learning to write and implement lesson plans.

The CRTWC lesson plan template can provide space to consider which social, emotional, and cultural anchors teachers will be working on in upcoming lessons in any content area. This does not mean attention is not given to the actual academic content, the skills needed by the student to succeed, or the materials needed for the class. It does mean, however, that the social, emotional, and cultural competencies necessary to be successful will also be addressed.

This might mean, for example, giving students the opportunity to work in groups on a math problem, along with a reminder about the importance of including and respecting all group members' contributions. After the group work, a member from each group then goes up to the board to share the group's thinking and response. Finally, after all the groups have shared their thinking, they engage in a discussion about what did and did not work. Within this lesson, the students will not only be learning a new math strategy but also practicing collaborative learning skills in a supportive academic environment, creating community by fostering engagement and hearing from individual voices, and cultivating perseverance.

Below is the lesson plan that Barbara Papamarcos used to teach a place value lesson to her third graders using the CRTWC Lesson Plan Template (see appendix A for the Lesson Plan Template).

Lesson Plan on Place Value

Lesson Rationale:

This lesson gives students an opportunity to examine the complex concept of place value and a deeper understanding of number sense, focusing on Common Core State Standards (CCSS). The anchor competencies of fostering self-reflection, promoting collaborative learning, and fostering a growth mindset will be the intentional anchor competencies focused on in this lesson.

Common Core State Standards:

www.cde.ca.gov/re/cc/:

- Use place value understanding and properties of operations to perform multidigit arithmetic.
- Construct viable arguments and critique reasoning of others.

English Language Development Standards:

Exchanging information and ideas with others through oral collaborative conversations on a range of social and academic topics.

English Language Development Objectives for Level 1 & 3:

- Level 1: The emerging student will contribute to the conversation/discussion by active listening and engaging when possible with yes/no or "what" questions. The response will be a short phrase or sentence. The student will have opportunity to illustrate or explain the answer in writing.
- Level 3: The expanding student will provide a longer response, possibly adding on relevant information and demonstrate turn taking in a class conversation. Student will use complete sentences to explain thinking.

Content/Subject Objective

(What do you want students to specifically learn as a result of this lesson?)

Students will be able to use place value and properties of operations to solve multidigit arithmetic.

Social, emotional, and cultural competencies

(What anchor competencies do students need to be successful in this lesson? How will they be taught, modeled, or reviewed?)

- Students and teacher will demonstrate self-reflection at the end of the lesson by recognizing how they influence behavior, show self-confidence, and talk about the lesson.
- Students and teacher will work on a growth mindset.
- Students and teacher will practice collaborative learning by listening to one another and building consensus.

Time (Pacing)	Step-by-step procedure (Instructional Sequence)	Where lesson plan elements are addressed (CCSS, ELD, Differentiation, Anchors, Formative & Summative Assessments)
10 min	**Introduction/hook** Teacher will use *One Grain of Rice*, a mentor text, to begin math lesson. This will illuminate the concept of place value and expand on it. The mentor text will use words the students are unfamiliar with, and teacher will slow lesson a bit to highlight vocabulary (raja, famine . . .). The concept of doubling will be highlighted. The concept of seeing large numbers, saying large numbers, identifying place value, and digit identification will be explored.	CCSS, ELD, CRI, Anchors
25 min	**Content instruction** Content instruction will be delivered using the district curriculum and focuses on the CCSS. Teachers will use the district provided materials. Whole class will practice place value and identifying which digit is in the tens place, hundreds place, and so on. Students will use number cards to make larger numbers. Teacher will work with small group to focus on expanding thinking and showing our thinking using words and illustration. Small group begins with discussion about digits and place value. Vocabulary is emphasized. Students will turn and talk to shoulder partner (need self-awareness, management skills, notice turn-taking, active listening, and gentle feedback). Students will use the phrase, "My partner says . . ." to encourage active listening and collaborative learning.	**CCSS to address the district curriculum** **ELD—Speaking and listening** **Anchors—foster self-reflection, confidence to share work, discuss the work, and collaborate with a partner (promote collaborative learning)**

	Continue on to using the place value combined with math operations to solve multidigit problems. Students are solving how to put marbles in bags. Students need to share their work in illustrations, with writing, and using numbers.	
5 min	**Closure/wrap-up/reflection** Students will complete the problem, explain it and share with each other. Also, students will share their learning from the day. Teacher will later reflect on how well the lesson went.	Foster self-reflection

In the spirit of engaging in self-reflection herself, Barbara wrote the following analysis of the lesson. Her reflection provides a glimpse into the thinking of a highly skilled teacher who is always interested in how to improve:

> This lesson did not go as I planned. . . . There was too much packed into one sitting and both the students and I were overwhelmed. It was also challenging to teach math, highlight the SEL skills and distinguish between the two. It needs to be more organic and integrated. My personal reflection is that I need to teach the content and be keenly aware of the students' learning needs. Then I can interject an anchor competency at that time. I need to be listening, responding and offering the anchor points when the time is right. I also need to know and understand which anchor competency is right for the moment. The reciprocal vulnerability is important to build a safe and more neutral environment. I can learn from the students and they can learn from me.

Observation Protocol

As is often pointed out in schools, what gets assessed gets addressed. This doesn't necessarily mean that teachers' use of the social, emotional, and cultural anchor competencies needs to be measured with high-stakes assessments (in fact, we strongly discourage such an approach). But, as with any skill needed by educators, ongoing observation and support is important to keep the anchor competencies on the radar, especially because teachers have such full plates. Again, we stress that this is not about asking teachers or administrators to do "one more thing" or work more, but rather supporting them to work differently and as effectively as possible for student success. For example, when a supervisor is debriefing with a teacher about the quality of feedback the teacher gave to students, the supervisor can include factors like the teacher's body language and whether her words emphasized a growth mindset along with comments about how clearly the teacher explained what more the student needed to do to meet the targeted academic standard.

In our experience, supervisors—whether in schools or teacher education programs—rarely look specifically for the application of the social, emotional, and cultural competencies. Nor do they generally have a common language to use when discussing the presence or absence of these practices in teaching. They tend to expect or request to see the teacher leading an SEL lesson with students about resolving conflict or doing group work, for example. But as we emphasize throughout this book, developing students' social, emotional, and cultural competencies must occur throughout the everyday instructional interactions between teachers and students. To focus only on a "growth mindset lesson" is to miss the real work of fostering a growth mindset.

One helpful tool is an observation protocol. Many principals and instructional coaches use such protocols to guide the kind of data they gather when observing teachers in the classroom. The Center for Reaching & Teaching the Whole Child originally developed an observation protocol tied to the Anchor Competencies Framework for use by supervisors who oversee student teaching placements during preservice teacher education. However, this protocol can be used by anyone observing and supporting a teacher at any stage of the career continuum.

Similar to the lesson plan template, the CRTWC observation protocol (see appendixes B and C for Observation Protocol Templates) provides a flexible structure for staying focused on the anchor competencies. It guides the supervisor in looking for and noting the teacher's use (or lack thereof) of specific strategies and incorporation of specific anchor competencies, and then in having a constructive debrief.

Table 3.2 is an example of the CRTWC observation protocol that a supervisor completed while observing a first-grade classroom teacher.

TABLE 3.2 Example of CRTWC observation protocol

ANCHORS/TEACHER MOVES (* indicates teacher move used in lesson)	SCRIPTING OF EVIDENCE
1. Builds trusting relationships ■ Teacher/student rapport evident* ■ Engages families ■ Encourages/engages in reciprocal vulnerability* ■ Employs trauma informed practices*	Teacher smiles frequently; makes jokes appropriate for 5- & 6-year-old children; gently asks students to do a number of tasks (e.g., take out your writing folders & research books). Students respond by being attentive & cooperative. Teacher shares that she struggles with drawing things that look as beautiful as in a book.
2. Fosters self-reflection ■ Recognizes & manages emotional reactions* ■ Examines biases ■ Explores identity	Teacher says, "And now I'm feeling a little nervous . . . because now it's time for me to do my picture . . . and I don't know how to draw this bat very well." She models how to share emotions in a calm way and asks students, "What can I do?" Teacher shared later that the class practices mindfulness activities each day.
3. Fosters growth mindset ■ Articulates affirming counter-narratives ■ Shifts to positive self-talk* ■ Makes connections between learning and the neuroscience of the brain	At the beginning of the lesson the teacher asks students to sit quietly and then says, "If you are sitting properly, please kiss your brain" (& she kisses her brain with her hand). Students respond with a menu of options to manage emotions such as, "Take a deep breath," "You can calm down," "It's OK," "Try your best." Teacher adds, "I can think about it—think about the pieces . . ." to add to their list of positive self-talk strategies.
4. Cultivates perseverance ■ Encourages students to embrace productive struggles* ■ Helps students set and monitor goals ■ Provides asset-based formative feedback	Teacher models perseverance by working slowly to fix "mistakes" she made in bat drawing. She asks students, "What else can I do?" (to improve drawing) and they respond, "You can make a beautiful oops!" Later teacher clarified that this is a book they read in class during the 1st week of school. Teacher models enthusiasm about learning and discusses the importance of taking risks as part of the growth process.
5. Creates community ■ Teacher/students send affirming messages to others* ■ Creates a culture of engagement* ■ Fosters individual voice* ■ Attends to status issues	Teacher says, "What can we do together . . . to learn together?" Students appear to feel very comfortable helping the teacher with her task by making suggestions in an orderly fashion (raising of hands). Teacher says, "Thank you, Jayla, they do have tails," encouraging students to feel part of the learning process. She refers to students by name and the whole class as "friends."

(continued)

TABLE 3.2 *(CONTINUED)*   Example of CRTWC observation protocol

ANCHORS/TEACHER MOVES (* indicates teacher move used in lesson)	SCRIPTING OF EVIDENCE
6. Promotes collaborative learning ■ Teacher/students practice reflective listening ■ Encourages students to engage in structured academic & social conversations ■ Practices building consensus	No evidence noted
7. Responds constructively across differences ■ Identifies & interrupts microaggressions ■ Builds students' capacity to make amends ■ Practices restorative justice	No evidence noted

AN EARLY START IS BEST

The habits and skills illustrated here take time to develop. And with social, emotional, and cultural competence, an early start is best, whether it's children getting started on the skills in early childhood, teachers establishing the foundation for classroom culture in the beginning of the year, or educators starting to develop the competencies when they are beginning their careers. In the next chapter, we explain why and how it makes sense to follow the old advice to begin at the beginning: teacher preparation.

CHAPTER 4

Laying the Groundwork in Preservice Teacher Education

ADVOCATES FOR INTEGRATING social, emotional, and cultural competence into the daily fabric of school life often call for more attention to this work in preservice teacher preparation—and rightly so.[1] After all, these programs establish the foundation of knowledge, skills, and habits of mind for the rest of a teacher's career. In this chapter, we will show how, in addition to its use in classrooms, the Anchor Competencies Framework can be used in teacher preparation programs to provide a common focus on social, emotional, and cultural competencies across all coursework and field experiences. The tools we shared in chapter 3, including the lesson plan template and observation protocol, help connect the framework to the entire program, making sure teacher candidates thoroughly practice teaching with a social, emotional, and cultural lens. In this chapter we will provide information about two additional tools, the course matrix and the program matrix, that can further ensure attention to the anchor competencies within individual courses and across the entire program.

THE ROLE OF PRESERVICE TEACHER EDUCATION

It is critical to understand the complicated process of teacher preparation and why it cannot be separated from what goes on directly in schools. To many people outside teacher education programs, what happens in these programs is a black box. While this chapter has direct application to those who work in teacher credential programs, the future teachers of our society will be better prepared if the work of universities, districts, states, and nonprofit organizations are tightly aligned. Additionally, when a credential program has strong partnerships with school districts in its local area, the university can serve as a catalyst for change in those schools. In our experience, cooperating teachers from districts who supervise teacher candidates can become leaders of this work in their own schools and districts. Ideally, the Anchor Competencies Framework can be part of a plan to align coursework, fieldwork, and instruction in a service area.

Teacher education programs are not all created equal, and many of these programs have room for improvement. Research suggests that one of the elements that makes programs effective is coherence. For example, programs whose coursework, field experiences, and supervision cohere around a common vision of culturally responsive teaching and socially just teaching are more effective than more fragmented programs.[2] Steven Athanases and Luciana de Oliveira studied graduates of such programs and found that most became advocates both in and out of their classrooms (e.g., setting up extra tutorials outside of class to meet diverse learning needs, speaking out to obtain needed resources for special-needs students, starting a bilingual parent group).[3] These teachers reported that they felt inclined to do so because their preparation program had emphasized the importance of advocacy and provided opportunities in their fieldwork to practice interceding on behalf of students and their families.

The Anchor Competencies Framework provides both a research-based process and a common set of competencies that can build greater consistency within teacher preparation programs. Additionally, because it brings together culturally responsive teaching practices with social and emotional learning, the framework enables graduates to start their careers with the ability to connect rather than silo these two critical areas of teaching.

In this chapter we describe both the work faculty can do with teacher candidates and the conditions needed within the programs to enable faculty to do that work, using the Anchor Competencies Framework as a guide. A program

FIGURE 4.1　The process of developing the lens

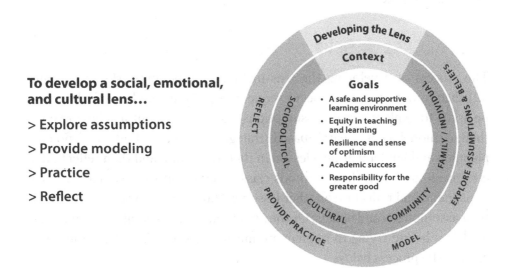

To develop a social, emotional, and cultural lens...

> Explore assumptions

> Provide modeling

> Practice

> Reflect

that integrates the framework throughout courses and fieldwork will develop new teachers who understand themselves and how their beliefs and assumptions influence the decisions they make, and who see how the actions they take in the classroom can either benefit or potentially harm their students. Critically, they will begin work in their own classrooms having had practice using the framework to guide their teaching.

Teacher preparation programs provide unique opportunities that some teachers will never have again. When else will they have the opportunity to deeply explore their own beliefs and assumptions about children, about teaching and learning, and about their role as teachers? When else will they have the opportunity to see powerful modeling of the social, emotional, and cultural lens in practice by both university faculty and cooperating teachers? And when else will they have an extended time to try out practice strategies with which they may be unfamiliar and perhaps even uncomfortable, and have the opportunity to reflect on and refine their work? In short, teacher preparation programs provide a one-of-a-kind opportunity to impact the thinking and behavior of thousands of new teachers pouring into our school systems each year in every state.

THE PROCESS OF DEVELOPING THE LENS: AN OVERVIEW

The process of developing the lens includes components (shown in figure 4.1) that do not necessarily occur sequentially. For example, candidates may be asked to explore certain assumptions and beliefs about teaching reading, then see modeling of research-based strategies in their methods class, practice planning and implementing a lesson in their fieldwork, and then reflect on its effectiveness back in their methods class. They might then be ready to plan, implement, and reflect on another lesson without going back to look again at their assumptions and beliefs. Or they might need to see multiple examples of modeling before trying to implement another lesson. We address these four parts of the process below.

Explore Assumptions and Beliefs

As described in chapter 2, exploring one's assumptions and beliefs is an essential first step for all professionals to integrate the social, emotional, and cultural lens into their practice. It is therefore important that we begin with a statement about our own beliefs and assumptions in this work at the college level, which include:

- Teachers are made, not born
- Teachers can develop a social, emotional, and cultural lens and use it effectively in the classroom
- A strong connection between coursework and fieldwork is necessary
- Along with family and community members, teachers are responsible for developing students' competencies in order to help them both achieve academically and thrive as individuals

Teachers are made, not born

As we stated earlier, we believe people go into teaching because they want to make a fundamental difference in the lives of children. If that is so, then what they need from a teacher preparation program are the skills and competencies to realize that goal. In the process, they will undoubtedly experience discomfort and challenges related to some prior assumptions and beliefs about teaching and learning, but that kind of thoughtful reflection is exactly what a preservice program should be encouraging.

Teachers can develop a social, emotional, and cultural lens and use it effectively in the classroom

In surveys, many teachers note that social and emotional competencies should have been addressed in their own preparation, but were not.[4] Therefore, from their perspective, as well as our own, the lens can be learned—and teachers-to-be want to learn it.

A strong connection between coursework and fieldwork is necessary

Making changes in teacher preparation programs requires targeting the two main components of these programs: coursework and field experiences. Done well, in a coordinated manner, these two parts work together to build a set of skills that teachers will be able to implement. But a never-ending challenge is providing consistency within and across these components. Most preparation programs, particularly large ones, are bifurcated. Teacher education faculty provide the foundations and methods courses, while adjunct university supervisors provide field supervision. Often these two parts of the program live in silos with little communication between them. In order for significant, systemic change to occur, however, the course- and fieldwork need to be integrally connected. Time for communication and professional development can lead to much-needed agreement on a common language, observation tools, lesson plan templates, and expected competencies of graduates.

Teachers share responsibility for developing students' social, emotional, and cultural competencies in order to help them both achieve academically and thrive as individuals

As we have described throughout this book, there is enough research from the neurosciences, psychology, and education to indicate that if children are to learn, grow, and thrive, both they and the educators who work with them need strong social, emotional, and cultural competencies. Too often, critics of social and emotional initiatives have argued that parents and community members are the ones who should assume responsibility for cultivating skills like managing emotional reactions and getting along well with peers. To this argument, we respond, "Yes, and . . . ." Developing young people's social, emotional, and cultural awareness and competence is everyone's responsibility. Just as it is now accepted that parents should promote young children's literacy skills at home, teachers should have the skills to respond constructively to bullying, anxiety, and other problems that our children need help addressing in classrooms, lunchrooms, school buses, and other places that are outside the watchful eyes of their parents. We do not advocate that parents abdicate responsibility for their children's social and emotional development, nor that teachers solve all of children's problems—quite the contrary, our approach helps teachers support young people in developing their own problem-solving skills.

To use the Anchor Competencies Framework effectively requires everyone involved in teacher preparation—university teacher educators, field supervisors, cooperating teachers, and candidates—to engage in the process of developing the social, emotional, and cultural lens outlined in the framework, beginning with exploring their beliefs and assumptions. No amount of modeling, practice, or reflection will lead to the kinds of instructional work we describe here unless educators deeply believe in its importance and appropriateness in the classroom. Every class at the university and each day in a student-teaching classroom can provide much-needed opportunities to explore and examine the beliefs and assumptions that guide the teacher's decision-making and interactions with students. We will provide descriptions of what exploring beliefs and assumptions looks like throughout this chapter.

Provide Modeling

Once educators have had the opportunity to explore, possibly challenge, and clarify the assumptions and beliefs that support implementation of the anchors, a significant amount of modeling is needed. Modeling the application of the anchors in teaching practice brings them to life. This modeling can occur across courses and field experience. In coursework, as will be described later in this chapter, professors can engage their candidates in lessons, show videos of teaching practice, or use written case studies to provide opportunities to see powerful models of teaching practice. The candidates can, in turn, try out these activities or strategies in their classrooms and reflect on their effectiveness.

During the field experience, both cooperating teachers and university supervisors can provide models of teaching with the anchor competencies in mind. In addition to continued modeling through opportunities to analyze videos and teaching cases, the supervisors can offer to do sample lessons in the teacher candidates' classrooms. Cooperating teachers provide an intense source of modeling as the candidates see them interacting with students every day for one semester or for a full academic year. Opportunities to observe the cooperating teacher modeling the anchors, followed by a debriefing on their observations, can be invaluable.

Provide Practice and Reflection

For those who will one day soon be teaching children and adolescents in their own classrooms, it is essential to have opportunities for ongoing practice and reflection in using the anchor competencies and the sample teacher moves throughout their time in the teacher preparation program. Just as doctors receive extensive opportunities to perform medical procedures under the supervision of seasoned experts before performing them independently, teachers should have ample opportunities to practice the social, emotional, and cultural competencies before being entrusted with the well-being and education of their own classes of students.

This process of exploring assumptions, modeling, and then providing many opportunities for practice and reflection may sound easier than it is. The reality is that everyone involved in preparing teachers must engage in some difficult and emotional work. Providing a safe, professional learning environment for everyone—those who prepare candidates and the candidates themselves—is essential. Teachers at all stages of professional learning need to be able to take risks and make mistakes, so that they can persevere, change, and increase their competence.[5]

INCORPORATING THE LENS IN COURSEWORK AND FIELD EXPERIENCE

In the remainder of this chapter, we describe ways and provide examples of how teacher education programs can incorporate modeling, practicing, and reflecting on the anchor competencies, while also exploring assumptions and beliefs. These kinds of practices should be incorporated into the two major components of teacher education programs: coursework and field experience placements.

The Anchor Competencies Integrated into Coursework

Coursework is the first requirement in most teacher preparation programs, and usually continues while candidates begin field experience placements in local classrooms to reinforce skills and build new ones. Coursework is therefore the logical place to begin building their social, emotional, and cultural lens.

Faculty should determine an early course or courses in which it makes sense to introduce the candidates to the Anchor Competencies Framework and the research basis for it. To ensure that faculty do not become overwhelmed, it is important to reassure them that developing the lens fully takes time, and that they will not be expected to master all elements of the framework and know how to include them in their courses after one or two professional development sessions. The same holds true for candidates—it will be important to reassure them, as well, that development of the lens takes time and practice. In fact, for both faculty and the candidates with whom they work, the goal is that they return to it over and over again throughout their teaching careers. Similarly, it is important to note that, just as we discourage social, emotional, and cultural competencies from being a series of brief lessons for K–12 students, we discourage this approach with teacher candidates. Initial instruction in the integration of social, emotional, and cultural competencies must be followed up, reinforced, and deepened by rich learning experiences throughout multiple courses and field placements. Below, we describe ways the anchor competencies can be further developed and reinforced in four common teacher preparation courses. These are merely examples of the many ways faculty can weave the lens into their teaching, however.

Math methods seminar

Math is not often seen as an area for building social, emotional, and cultural learning, but in fact, math teaching is ripe with such opportunities. Many students—and even teachers, especially those at the elementary level—feel anxious and negative about math. The anchor competencies are helpful for reducing anxiety and increasing the ability to persevere and succeed at math, especially the anchor competencies of building trusting relationships, creating community, fostering growth mindset, fostering self-reflection, cultivating perseverance, and promoting collaborative learning.

One example of how to build these anchor competencies in a math methods course comes from San José State University professor Patricia Swanson. Swanson is a math specialist, but she is well aware of the discomfort many students and teachers feel with the subject. To change those perceptions and empower candidates to teach math with confidence and enthusiasm, Swanson made attention to the social, emotional, and cultural competencies an explicit part of her teaching. The following examples of activities in which Swanson engaged her candidates shows, in particular, the interaction between self-awareness and problem-solving in mathematics.

Inspired by an article describing how writing metaphors can be a powerful assessment of students dispositions toward mathematics, Swanson asked candidates to explore their assumptions and beliefs about mathematics by writing their own math metaphors comparing mathematics to a vegetable, fruit, or animal.[6] Student responses have included the following:

> "I would say a mosquito, because whatever you do to try to get away from it, it always comes back. It's annoying because you hate taking math every year, and whatever you try to do to stop it, it always fails."
>
> "Tiger. Because I don't like tigers: ferocious and [easy] to fear—just like math with too much thinking and hard-to-solve problems. It really hurts my brain to think about all those problems that I cannot solve."
>
> "Vegetables are good for you, and so is mathematics for daily things. It is needed for life. Some people like it, and some people don't, but you still need it to live a healthy life."

The candidates have fun sharing their metaphors and become aware that they are not alone in their negative beliefs, assumptions, and nervousness about math. Through this activity, Swanson models the integration of several anchor competencies. She has begun to build trusting relationships among herself and the candidates and create community among the class. She also fosters self-reflection in candidates, prompting them to reflect on their beliefs about teaching and learning mathematics. She then begins to foster a growth mindset and cultivate perseverance by letting them know that they are all in this together and that using positive self-talk and having opportunities to solve problems together will promote everyone's success.

In another class session, Swanson tackles the issue of how to help students learn to grapple with challenging word problems, again starting by addressing the teacher candidates' own beliefs and assumptions about what they can and cannot do in the field of mathematics.[7] She begins by showing them (while reading aloud with a certain level of drama), the following multistep problem taken directly from a sixth-grade math textbook:

> The density of a substance is the ratio of its mass to its volume, written as a unit rate.
>
> A. Calculate: A 500 cubic centimeter sample of sea water has a mass of 514 grams. Find its density.
> B. Calculate: A 300 cubic centimeter sample of an iceberg has a mass of 267 grams. Find its density.
> C. Compare: Which is denser, sea water or an iceberg? Explain why your answer is reasonable.[8]

She then asks the candidates to describe their immediate emotional reaction to this problem and describe what they say to themselves when they encounter a problem like this. Responses typically indicate that many (although not all) preservice teachers feel incompetent and stressed by multistep word problems. Here are a few she heard in one class:

"Oh crap, this might take a while!"

"Fear. Math is not a subject I feel confident in doing or teaching."

"This problem makes me feel frustrated and disappointed in my own math skills."

"This is intriguing . . . challenge accepted!"

"Help!!! I tested out of math all through my undergraduate courses, and I'm not happy about having to take it now."

"Will this class be too much for me?"

Swanson then shares with them the responses of sixth-grade students when she asked the same questions about the same problem, and the candidates see that the responses are remarkably similar:

"I am frustrated and confused. But I also feel like my teacher hasn't taught this."

"I can't do it. I do not know what to do."

"It triggered the run response in my brain."

She brainstorms with candidates the strategies they use to walk themselves through difficult problems, and the candidates discuss how to model and teach these strategies to children. Finally, she shares sixth graders' reflections on how using strategies like taking deep breaths to calm down, working collaboratively, going step-by-step, or simply slowing down and rereading the problem, helped them to engage with the problem and ultimately solve it.

"I could have done this really quickly if I wasn't freaking out!"

"If I paid attention to what I knew instead of freaking out I would have actually gotten the problem."

"It was easy if I just didn't freak out."

In many cases, both teacher candidates and sixth-grade students realize that the math skills required for the problem are actually quite basic, and that it was the multistep label and the language of the word problem that made it intimidating.

Swanson often asks candidates to adapt these kinds of lessons to their field placement classrooms, providing candidates with the opportunity for practice and reflection. The candidates will then come back to class and share their comfort level with doing this activity, what they learned about their students, and their reflections on beginning to build the anchor competencies in their students.

Within these activities, Swanson moves her candidates through the entire process of developing social, emotional, and cultural competencies by exploring their beliefs and assumptions, modeling, and providing them with opportunities for practice and reflection—and she does so within a content area not usually associated with social, emotional, and cultural work. In the initial activity, she has the candidates explore their beliefs and assumptions about the subject of math and their competence to teach it. She is modeling how to build trust, create community, promote a growth mindset, and persevere, and giving them the opportunity to practice and reflect on those strategies.

She also incorporates several other anchor competencies by using some of the sample teacher moves in the framework. She uses the teacher move of reciprocal vulnerability to promote a trusting relationship, saying how the problem initially made her take a step back. Then, by asking the students to share their feelings about their capacity to do the problem, she gives them the opportunity to see that they are not alone in feeling tentative and unsure. Further, she fosters a growth mindset among those doubters by shifting self-talk and sending affirming messages. She tells them that they have conquered much academically on their way to becoming teachers and that, together, they will solve this problem as well. She has them work in cooperative groups of four to identify what they think they know about the problem and then share suggestions across groups. All along the way, she encourages the candidates to breathe and persevere, or as one candidate put it, take the stance of "challenge accepted."

Literacy methods seminar

Literacy instruction presents another valuable, and often more obvious, opportunity for teachers to apply the anchors and attend to students' social and emotional skills, using an explicitly culturally responsive approach to teaching. University faculty can teach candidates how to be intentional and explicit in integrating anchors into their teaching of literacy practices, providing an essential foundation for the achievement of literacy standards. Literature, both fiction and nonfiction, provides virtually limitless opportunities to consider characters' perspectives and emotions, explore cultural differences and related topics like implicit bias, and discuss how to handle social conflicts and make tough decisions.

Consider the following dilemma that came up during a typical literacy methods course. The professor was focusing this particular seminar on the need to help candidates learn how to assess the appropriateness of literature selections for their classes using Louise Derman-Sparks' "Guide for Selecting Anti-Bias Children's Books."[9] This guide encourages teachers to pay attention to the importance of providing diverse literature, including characters with whom students of various cultural, linguistic, religious, and family backgrounds can identify, as a critical part of culturally responsive teaching practices. The professor spent a significant part of the session talking with the students about how to analyze literature for diversity.

During the discussion, it emerged that some candidates were intimidated about using literature from outside their own cultural and/or linguistic reference points, even though they believed in the importance of doing so. Some were worried about using books with phrases in languages they didn't speak, for fear of looking foolish or incompetent, particularly to those students more proficient in that language, or reading stories using Black English for fear that some parents would complain that children were being taught nonstandard English. These were candidates who had clearly indicated a passion and commitment to supporting diverse learners. The fact that they brought up their discomfort publicly showed that the professor had built a trusting relationship with her students and created a safe and supportive classroom community. Had she not set these anchors down at the beginning of the semester and continued to build them each week, some candidates would likely have listened and nodded in agreement with what she suggested, even though they did not actually feel comfortable enough to use diverse literature in their teaching.

The professor's first step was to acknowledge the candidates' discomfort, not dismiss it (continuing to reinforce a trusting relationship with them). She engaged in the teacher move of reciprocal vulnerability by sharing with them her own discomfort in reading certain children's stories. She told them how she sometimes had to practice quite a bit before feeling comfortable enough to read certain stories in front of a class. She then modeled reading a story with which she had initially felt insecure because of several phrases in the book that were in Spanish. Next she gave them the following assignment that included increasing levels of difficulty of practice and reflection: As part of the preparation for the next class, students were to choose a book that they felt insecure about using, whether because of language issues or content, and write in their journal why they were uncomfortable using this particular book. They were also asked to practice reading the story in the privacy of their own homes. In class the following week, they would read the story to a partner and reflect on their current level of comfort with the book. They were then encouraged to share their experience and resulting feelings with their classmates, promoting a continuing sense of community, growth mindset, and perseverance in the class.

After this low pressure experience, the professor asked them to read the same story to the students they were teaching in their field experiences, again writing about how they felt ahead of time and how they felt afterward. In the process of doing this, the professor was intent on helping the candidates explore their original assumptions and beliefs both about their own capabilities and what was appropriate content for children.

If these issues had not been discussed and dealt with in her class, the likelihood that candidates would have talked about them elsewhere would have been slim to nonexistent. As a result, the chances that these candidates would use some of the literature she recommended would have been extremely low, and their students—not only those in their field placement classes but perhaps throughout their careers—would have lost opportunities to connect with and see themselves represented in literature, which we know is important for success in literacy and beyond.[10]

Providing a strong connection between discussing assumptions, beliefs, and modeling in the literacy methods course, and providing opportunities for practice and reflection in that course and in the field can make all the difference in whether or not those candidates will actually enact these practices once in their own classrooms.

Classroom management seminar

Classroom management is one of the areas of greatest concern and challenge for many new and future teachers, and it is also one of the areas most clearly suited to cultivating and applying the social, emotional, and cultural lens. However, traditional classroom management courses are often focused on controlling students rather than building their self-regulation skills, and they often rely on outmoded models of behaviorism—using rewards and punishments—rather than leveraging the large body of research on the benefits of social and emotional learning and culturally responsive teaching practices.

Decades of research show that extrinsic reinforcement—engaging in a desired behavior to receive a reward or avoid a punishment—may appear effective in the short term, but in the long term it doesn't build skills and can actually decrease people's motivation to act in a desired way when left to their own devices.[11] Such reinforcements can be beneficial for teaching very basic lessons about right and wrong, but when used as the primary means of reinforcing behavior expectations, they tend to backfire in the long run. Studies in labs and classrooms show that when people get used to rewards and then the rewards are taken away, they are less likely to enjoy the tasks for which they received rewards or persist in the face of challenges. They may also be less likely to develop the habits and strategies to regulate themselves. This becomes particularly relevant when students who are accustomed to rewards go off to college or jobs where they don't receive such rewards, and they suddenly lose their motivation and realize they don't have the skills they need to manage their time, seek out help, or keep trying when a task is very difficult.[12]

Another problem with typical classroom management courses is that they often fail to consider context. In particular, they don't often address cultural differences in behavior or assumptions about children from diverse backgrounds, therefore doing little to disrupt troubling patterns of racial disparities in school disciplinary actions. As early as preschool, African American children, especially boys, are more likely than their peers to be suspended and even expelled, even for minor behavioral infractions.[13] In addition, some charter schools that serve primarily populations of color have been criticized for their harsh behavioral codes, such as requirements that students "track" the teacher at all times with their eyes and ears, and sharp punishments for even minor infractions, like failing to tuck in a shirt or looking out the window during class.[14] The purported goal of these approaches is to give students who have historically been marginalized more access to a high school diploma and college enrollment through "high expectations" and "no excuses" for academic failure. Reformers leading this movement claimed to be sending the message that students need not be derailed by forces external to schools, like poverty, violence, and family instability, and that focusing on those problems was tantamount to making excuses for the failure on the part of adults to set high expectations and do the hard work of instruction, and on the part of students to buckle down and do the work.

But there are a number of limitations to this approach, which have become more and more apparent over time. First, strict behavior codes and zero-tolerance policies have pushed out of these schools some of the students most in need of support, either through disciplinary action or because students drop out.[15] Second, strict behavioral codes don't build students' self-regulation skills like time management, help-seeking, and delaying gratification. That becomes particularly problematic when students get to college and are expected to be responsible for their own academic paths.[16] Students who do everything for an award or a dollar at the school store, or who are solely aiming to avoid detention or expulsion, quickly lose those reinforcements in a setting like college or the workplace. Perhaps not surprisingly, several no-excuses charter schools have realized that although they got most or all of their students into college, few of those students were getting through college. Many found themselves lost and overwhelmed, and dropped out of school with no diplomas and mountains of debt.[17]

There is another, harder to quantify problem with no-excuses schools: they are often largely attended by children of color and staffed by White teachers and administrators. Some have criticized these schools for imposing a vision of what a group of privileged White people think a "successful" school for low-income children of color should look like, or of reproducing a larger societal pattern in which White people are in charge and people of color are expected to be subordinate or face harsh punishments even for minor infractions.[18]

Using the Anchor Competencies Framework as a foundation can change these patterns before they start, by shaping teachers' assumptions about student behavior and, consequently, their response to it. From paying attention to the anchor of fostering self-reflection about implicit bias, to creating community that affirms each student's voice and makes room for varying perspectives, to responding constructively across differences, there are many ways faculty can incorporate the framework in classroom management courses and support candidates to develop students' self-regulation skills rather than just punishing them.

One way the Anchor Competencies Framework can be applied in classroom management seminars is through the use of a student case study project, in which candidates select a student who is challenging in class, identify and explore their beliefs and assumptions about that student, gather data on the student using a guide from the professor, and ultimately try alternative ways of responding to and supporting that student. Student case studies are commonly required in teacher preparation programs and completed during student teaching placements.

Nancy has used this structure to create a semester-long assignment that provides candidates with practice using the social, emotional, and cultural lens to better understand students who challenge them. Within the first couple of weeks of the classroom management course, she asks candidates to identify a student in their field placement class with whom they feel the least comfortable and the most challenged. She asks them to write down assumptions and beliefs they have about the student, for example about their home life, their interest in school, and their capabilities. Over the course of the semester, Nancy then engages the candidates in a series of data-gathering activities about the student. These activities include observing the student on the playground during recess and lunch, in the classroom, and in other classes like art and library. If possible, they look at the cumulative file accompanying the child each year and talk to the child's previous teacher. They also examine student work samples with another candidate, using a student work protocol.[19]

Nancy intentionally scaffolds the process of developing the anchor framework lens (exploring assumptions and beliefs, modeling, and practice and reflection). After each data-gathering activity, candidates spend some time in their seminar fostering self-reflection by talking about what they learned and how it is informing their thinking about the student. During the course of this data gathering, candidates often learn information about the student that may be unknown or unaddressed by anyone else at the school.

For example, one Latino student in the fourth grade had previously attended four other schools, all of which used different programs for English language learners. The candidate indicated that this information totally changed how he looked at the student's struggles in class. The candidate started thinking about how to create more support for the student as he was learning English because he no longer assumed that this student "just wasn't trying very hard."

Another candidate found out that her third-grade student, who was acting out in class, had lost her mother to cancer when she was in first grade. No one had paid attention to how this loss had traumatized the child and was likely impacting her ability to concentrate in class. The candidate shared this information with her cooperating teacher. Instead of seeing the student's behavior as purposefully challenging their authority, they developed empathy for the student. This did not mean that they would now accept the student's inappropriate behavior, but it did change their focus from the use of punitive behavior management strategies to supporting the student by giving her needed space to experience and express her feelings and helping her with coping strategies. This meant they put their energy into using strategies to build a trusting relationship with the student and encourage self-reflection.

"A few of my [assumptions] about [the student] changed: One of them was . . . that our relationship couldn't be improved and he would never stop testing me. [This assumption] changed with my implementation of the 2/10 Activity which built a positive relationship between us, and helped diminish how much and often he would test boundaries with me."

(teacher candidate journal entry)

The last major case study activity that occurs toward the end of the semester is very challenging for candidates, but very powerful. They are required to do the "two/ten" activity: talking with their case study student for two minutes each day for ten days about topics unrelated to school or their behavior—topics such as pets, sports, or favorite music.[20] Many candidates exhibit significant reticence about doing this activity because of their discomfort with the student.

However, in almost every case, this activity fundamentally changes the candidate's relationship with the student. Often the information teachers find out during these brief chats, such as that the child has just lost a pet, or that someone in their family is ill, helps the teacher develop empathy for the child and therefore respond to him or her more positively in class.

In another example, one kindergarten teacher candidate had started becoming very annoyed because a little boy in his class was always hanging on him physically. Initially, the teacher made an assumption that the parents weren't giving enough attention to the child. However, in the course of doing the two/ten activity, he found out that the little boy's father was currently incarcerated. That piece of information changed the teacher's assumptions and beliefs about the child, and consequently his strategy for working with him. Instead of being annoyed, the candidate talked with his cooperating teacher about how to better connect with the child. Together, they planned and began to implement small steps to help this student feel cared for and comforted, including inviting the child to lunch with the teacher weekly for a month and choosing him to become a teacher helper after school, cleaning the boards and putting classroom materials away. The teacher candidate noted that the child gradually became less in need of the teacher's attention during class time.

By prompting teacher candidates to gather data on a student they might otherwise have missed and to reflect on that data, the student case study approach propels them to try teacher moves and strategies that help them build relationships where little or none had existed. And, by requiring students to practice talking to children with whom they feel uncomfortable, they develop a closer rapport and more willingness to engage with that student and other challenging students in the future. The end result of this effort in just about every case is a decrease in student misconduct and an increase in the teacher wanting to work with the child.

It is extremely important to do the kind of thoughtful work about assumptions and beliefs before attempting to address challenging behavior with interventions when bridging racial, ethnic, and cultural gaps. For example, many teachers, not having lived in a place where they had to go to school and listen to a language they did not know, do not understand why an English language learner may be acting out in class. They don't know what it is like to have to sit for hours every day, not fully understanding what is going on. As a consequence they may interpret student behaviors such as shouting out or fidgeting as a "won't" rather than as a "can't."

Consider the following story. During her work as a university supervisor, Nancy observed the unfortunate consequences of a teacher not doing the hard work of exploring assumptions and practicing uncomfortable moves. She was visiting a third-grade classroom and noticed that there was one student with whom the cooperating teacher was having difficulty. During full-group lessons on the front carpet, this student, a Latino, always sat in the very back. Periodically he would shout out answers or try to distract the students sitting around him. During each observation, Nancy noticed that the teacher would start by asking the student to settle down. The student would initially try but eventually go back to engaging in disruptive behaviors. The teacher's next step was to send him to the first-grade classroom next door as a punishment. Shaming him was clearly part of the plan, hoping that would cause him to rethink his behavior. This pattern went on for several weeks. Two months later, when Nancy came to the classroom, the teacher candidate told her that the student had proceeded to disrupt the first-grade classroom as well, so that teacher had sent him to the office. The student ended up being suspended from school.

Prior to the suspension, Nancy had worked individually with this student to support him during independent reading time. In that one-to-one situation, he appeared focused and attentive. However, in the whole-class lessons, language became an issue for him. Since he could not understand what was going on, he gave up trying and became bored, perhaps feeling frustrated or even invisible—all of this leading to his misbehavior.

Had the teacher done a little observation of the student on the playground to gather information about his social life at school and done the two/ten activity with him, she could have explored her assumptions about this student, revised them, and employed moves to develop a relationship with this student. She could have learned more about his background and what was giving him difficulty during the group lessons, acknowledged how challenging it could be, and asked him what she could do to support him. She could also have provided a counternarrative to the larger societal belief that people who speak Spanish as their native language are low status by sending an affirming message about how awesome it was that he was becoming bilingual in Spanish and English. She could have read stories to the whole class about students who come to school speaking a language other than English and given him a chance to shine as someone with that experience, raising his status vis-à-vis the other students. The teacher also could have promoted perseverance by creating more one-on-one time with him and given him visuals to follow during whole-group instruction to accommodate his needs. Had the teacher taken this alternate path, that student's trajectory could have been completely different—both the student and the teacher would have likely thrived and experienced success.

Using this story or others like it as a case study for discussion can give preservice candidates the chance to think differently and avoid making the mistakes made by the teacher in the story. Classroom management seminars are a valuable time to do this work and focus on using the framework to prevent and address behavior challenges. In fact, many of the students who engaged in the data-gathering activities Nancy used with her students reported that the target student was less likely to be disruptive in class and more likely to engage with the teacher, and that the teacher felt much more disposed to work with the student.

For an additional example of the CRTWC Lesson Plan used in a secondary History Methods seminar, see sidebar.

The role of cultural context in these courses

The course activities previously described were neither created nor implemented in a vacuum. Consider the lesson on the use of diverse literature in the classroom. The professor spent the initial part of the session discussing criteria that could be used to assess whether the literature used in the classroom represents the diversity of the society. This lesson addressed the need for students to see representations of themselves in what they read. Prior to this particular session, the teacher candidates had been asked to scan the books available in their field classrooms. Many of the candidates indicated either a lack of representative stories or a kind of segregation of literature, in which the stories about characters of color were placed in a Multicultural Books section while the rest of the books were in another section. One gay teacher candidate noticed that his classroom did not have a single book with LGBTQ characters

LESSON PLAN:
USING SOCRATIC SEMINARS IN A UNITED STATES HISTORY METHODS COURSE

Wendy Thowdis, SJSU Social Science Undergraduate Teacher Preparation Program

Learning objectives: Students will be able to

1. identify the benefits and challenges of using Socratic Seminars/deliberative discourse for students to master historical content and practice Common Core skills;

2. identify specific steps for facilitating effective Socratic Seminars;

3. articulate the social, emotional, and cultural anchor competencies and teacher moves that need to be explicitly modeled/taught for students to be able to engage in structured academic conversations with diverse partners; and

4. integrate Socratic Seminars into a lesson plan to demonstrate an understanding of what it means to "Develop a social, emotional, and cultural lens" (explore assumptions, model, practice, reflect).

Length: Two 3-hour classes

Prior learning: We studied the Founding Era, which included a simulation around the question: "Was the American Revolution inevitable?" Students read primary source documents representing White colonists (Patriots & Loyalists), free and enslaved Blacks, Indigenous people, and women. The unit culminated in an exploration of the US Constitution and the political life of the 1780's. The final question students answered in this unit was: "Is the Constitution a pro-slavery document?" We also have been identifying the anchor competencies and teacher moves needed to create a safe and supportive learning environment, using the process of developing the lens outlined in the Anchor Competencies Framework.

Preparation for final exam socratic seminar: Students will use this lesson as practice for their Final Exam, which is a performance assessment.

DAY ONE

Growth of slavery in America: Developing the social, emotional, and cultural lens

I. Gallery walk: Analysis of primary source documents about slavery; on large Post-its write initial reactions to images or text and connections to the United States/world today.

II. Explore assumptions by connecting to the historical thinking skills we have been discussing all semester

  A. *Developing historical empathy* (How can we appreciate the past on its own terms?)

  B. *Understanding ethical dimensions of history* (What responsibilities do we have to those who have been oppressed? What, if any, reparations do we owe? What can we learn from the past?)

  C. *Causality & chronology* (Who is responsible for telling the stories of history? How can we broaden the scope of historical memory to include collective memory?)

III. Model/teach with an interactive lecture; focus question: "Which view of slavery better served the interests of the United States between 1800 and 1860?"

A. **Outline of lecture:** Interactive timeline of the history of slavery in the Americas; the experience of slavery; distinctive features of southern slavery; pro-slavery & anti-slavery positions

B. **Social Studies pedagogy:** A.P.P.A.R.T.S. & Expert Jigsaw—primary source document analysis; Word clouds—formative assessment; Gallery walk—create a culture of engagement; note-taking outline—Tier 3 vocabulary terms & gathering of evidence; "Aha moments"—reflections

DAY TWO

Homework reading: Hess, Diana (March, 2004). *Discussion in Social Studies: Is it Worth the Trouble?* Social Education 68 (2), pp. 151–155. National Council for the Social Studies.

https://www.socialstudies.org/publications/socialeducation/march2004/discussion-in-social-studies-is-it-worth-the-trouble

Discussion questions:

1. According to the author, what are the benefits of conducting deliberative discussions in a classroom?
2. What are key characteristics of effective discussions?
3. How can a teacher create a safe learning environment for students to feel comfortable engaging in these deep discussions?

I. Introduce what is a Socratic Seminar?
   A. Show video *The Power of Socratic Seminars in the Classroom* & have students complete the video worksheet
   B. Discuss handout: *Socratic Seminar Sentence Stems*
   C. Describe the parameters of our in-class Socratic Seminar: taking on the roles of teacher and student.

II. Practice: Students engage in a Socratic Seminar as practice for their final exam Socratic Seminar
   A. Preparation for our practice Socratic Seminar on slavery question
      1. In groups of 3, complete your notecards with clear position statements, at least 3 reasons to support your position, and 5 quotations from the primary sources we have studied that can be used as textual evidence during the seminar.
      2. Review the *Socratic Seminar Sentence Stems* and select at least 5 to use during the seminar from a variety of categories.
      3. Select 1 person from your group to participate in the practice seminar; the rest will act as coaches & observers.
   B. Conducting a practice Socratic Seminar
      1. Review the rules & procedures for seminars; hand out 2 small Post-its per participant in the inner circle; encourage participants to use their notecards and share positions, reasons, and quotes as evidence.

2. Outer circle will be observers and complete the Observer Write-Up. They will also act as coaches during a break in the seminar.

3. Begin the seminar by posing the essential question: "Which view of slavery better served the interests of the United States between 1800 and 1860?"

III. Reflect: Post-seminar discussion questions:

A. How did it feel to participate in this seminar?

B. What did you learn about (content, process, and yourself in these situations)?

C. Which anchor competencies & teacher moves would you have to teach/model prior to this lesson to help your students feel safe to engage in seminars?

D. How might you incorporate this into a content lesson?

and put together a list of possible titles to address that gap and supplement what was currently in his classroom.

This attention to representation of student context needs to extend to all kinds of student identities and experiences, such as being adopted or living in a transracial family. The extent to which the teacher takes the time to learn about individual students and their families and to ensure they feel seen and represented will affect the degree to which all students within the class feel a part of the learning community.

Looking at the math methods lesson, the professor clearly wanted to develop a growth mindset about math in the teacher candidates. Even though these were graduate students who had already experienced significant academic success in order to get where they were, they brought negative internal narratives about math with them to teaching. What about the students they would be teaching? Those students might bring even more negative narratives about math and their own competence, especially those from traditionally marginalized groups, who might have negative narratives playing on an ongoing tape in their brains.

For example, in our society, Spanish is viewed as a low status language and much of the public rhetoric today reinforces that Latinx students themselves are of low status.[21] So when they come into classrooms, the teacher cannot just talk about developing a growth mindset. She needs to understand the narratives that students carry with them that do not support development of a growth mindset. Then she needs to provide examples of counternarratives to what they may be hearing and thinking about their own competence. Activities like talking with students in the two/ten activity may provide information about the internal narratives about self-worth and competence that they bring to class and open a window for counternarratives. An informed teacher is well positioned to talk with students about how they can use the cognitive skills they have developed through their multiple languages and apply them to the challenge of learning math.

Ensuring anchor competencies are addressed in all coursework
In surveys we have conducted, and in our own experience with university departments, we have observed that many faculty address social, emotional, and cultural competencies within specific courses, but neglect to look at or know how these competencies should be woven throughout the program.[22] For example, faculty will say they have addressed growth mindset within the educational psychology course, culturally responsive teaching practices within the multicultural and second-language learning classes, and how to create a classroom community in the classroom management seminar. But research shows this is not how the competencies develop—either for adults or children. The competencies need to be addressed *across* courses and throughout the fieldwork.[23]

With all of these potential opportunities to reinforce the framework—not to mention the dozens of other goals and requirements of teacher education programs—how can program directors and faculty make sure their efforts to cultivate the social, emotional, and cultural lens are coherent and building competencies in an intentional progression? What if every faculty member decides to focus on promoting collaborative learning and no one addresses cultivating perseverance or fostering growth mindset? Worse, what if everyone forgets to use the framework at all?

The Center for Reaching & Teaching the Whole Child created a simple tool, the Anchor Competencies Program Matrix, to help faculty and leadership teams plan where and when in the program the competencies will be addressed.

The program matrix provides space to note in which courses, seminars, and other opportunities (such as voluntary workshops) each of the anchor competencies and core steps will be addressed. (An example is provided in table 4.1.) Working together, program directors and other faculty members fill in the boxes identifying where in the program each of the seven anchor competencies is explicitly taught. They can then discuss potential changes across courses and fieldwork to create more coherence. We have found that taking small programmatic steps each year is ultimately more effective than trying to modify everything at once.

No one course can or should be expected to address every competency. Certain faculty will feel more or less comfortable with different anchor competencies and will see more or fewer opportunities to address them in their course(s). That's perfectly normal, and programs are more likely to be successful with the framework if they build on those preferences as starting places.

Initiating the process to revise courses and the program
Usually, teacher educators start by identifying where they are already addressing some of the anchor competencies within their own courses, and then decide where they want to add further work on the competencies. Sometimes this individual faculty work is done independently, at least in the first year, as the professor works on modifying their own course(s) and on getting buy-in from the department or college leadership. Sometimes, where leadership buy-in is already in place, as at the University of Dayton, individual faculty work on course revision occurs in parallel with work on the entire program. We recommend mapping out where and when the process of developing the lens and the anchor competencies will be addressed in each course and throughout the program.

For example, at one of the SJSU teacher educator department retreats, faculty were asked to come with their course syllabi and notes indicating which anchor competencies were addressed in their courses. The department chair created an Anchor Competencies Program Matrix on butcher paper that covered a whole wall. Faculty were first asked to write on individual Post-its what they were doing related to the anchor competencies in their courses. They then went up to the program matrix and put their Post-its in the appropriate cells (see appendix E for the Program Matrix Template). After everyone had finished, the faculty had a discussion about which anchors were being addressed and how. While the candidates learned about growth mindset in their educational psychology course, were they getting an opportunity to practice this competency using appropriate strategies in their field experience? Similarly, while several faculty modeled mindfulness activities as a teaching strategy to foster self-reflection (addressing the teacher move of managing emotional reactions), it was not clear if anyone was going into depth about the teacher move of exploring identity. After going through this process and analyzing the results, the whole faculty—both professors and field supervisors—were able to identify possible programmatic changes to ensure coverage of all the anchors.

We provide an example of the work that is ongoing at the University of Dayton. There, faculty who participated as Fellows in the CRTWC Teacher Educator Institute (TEI) started the process of integrating the anchor competencies into their own courses and served as a leadership team to work with faculty on program revisions. The leadership team created and implemented a yearlong plan to introduce the faculty to the Anchor Competencies Framework (see sidebar). Many of the strategies they used with the faculty were ones that they had seen modeled, had practiced, and had reflected on as Fellows at the TEI.

UNIVERSITY OF DAYTON IMPLEMENTATION PROCESS
2017–2018 ACADEMIC YEAR

Role of team leadership members:

Team members piloted integration of Anchor Competencies Framework and anchor competencies into their courses.

Team members planned and facilitated whole faculty professional development as outlined below.

Whole faculty:

August

We gave an hour and a half presentation at the Department of Teacher Education August faculty meeting. The presentation included:

- An overview of our team's involvement with the Center for Reaching & Teaching the Whole Child (CRTWC) this year and their Institute's goals and objectives:
  - Develop a common language related to anchors
  - Understand the connection between Social and Emotional Learning (SEL) and Culturally Responsive Teaching (CRT) and begin to develop a social, emotional, and cultural lens to guide teaching practices

- - Understand the anchor competencies, outcomes, teacher actions/behaviors needed to explicitly integrate anchors
  - Understand and implement anchor competencies as an academic intervention to support teacher candidates and enable teacher candidates to utilize strategies within their own professional development
  - Integrate anchors into Teacher Education (EDT) courses and programs
- The case for SEL given outcomes / benefits for student performance and behavior and the need for both K–12 students and teachers to have anchor competencies
- A description of the social, emotional, and cultural anchor competencies
- Exploration of the anchor competencies and possible teacher moves
- A mindfulness exercise

September

Team presentation at Department of Teacher Education faculty meeting included:

- Mindfulness exercise
- Review of anchor competencies and teacher moves
- Viewing and discussion of the *Run Response* video of Patty Swanson in math methods course with teacher candidates

October

Team presentation at Department of Teacher Education faculty meeting included:

- Reminder of the Institute's goals and objectives
- Definitions of CRT from Dr. Geneva Gay and Dr. Ladson-Billings, review of anchor competencies, and consideration of which teacher moves support culturally responsive teaching and why
- Viewing of Moises video and discussion of the following questions:
  - What assumptions might have informed the teacher's thinking and actions during this lesson? What do you think she "believed" was true about Moises, the abilities of the rest of the class, and the learning process?
  - Which anchor competencies would the teacher have had to teach, model, and practice since the beginning of the year to lead to different student behaviors in her class? Which teacher moves could the teacher have made during the lesson?

November

Dr. Nancy Markowitz's presentation and discussion with faculty.

January

- The team shared resources available at our Curriculum Materials Center that support integration of Anchor Competencies Framework into our curriculum
- Team reported on the January institute in California and framework goals for the semester.

- Team members also reported on upcoming scholarly and professional development initiatives including a proposal for NAEYC presentation

March

At Department of Teacher Education faculty meeting, faculty watched the Bear video and discussed narratives and counter narratives (45 minutes).

April

- Faculty discussed value of the Anchor Competencies Framework to candidates and their future students
- The faculty reached consensus to integrate the anchor competencies throughout our teacher education curriculum
- Team members shared how they have been integrating teaching the anchor competencies in their classes

May

- Faculty led "fishbowl" discussion by common or similar course faculty (e.g., EDT 110: Professional aspects of teaching; Second-year child and adolescent development courses; EDT 340: Teaching diverse students in inclusive settings)
- Discussed the importance of having a common language to facilitate sharing across and within program areas as we move forward with integration of anchor competencies
- Program teams completed draft Anchor Competencies Program Matrix
- Faculty began crosswalk between anchor competencies and CPAST, the Ohio student teaching evaluation protocol

Future plans

Faculty will:

- review and refine draft anchor competency matrix
- consider updating their syllabi to include anchor competencies
- begin embedding anchor competencies into their individual classes

The Anchor Competencies Integrated into Fieldwork Experiences

The field experience is a critical part of every teacher preparation program. To date, attention to the social, emotional, and cultural lens has been particularly rare in fieldwork. The Anchor Competencies Framework can help change that. Much of the suggested modeling, practice, and reflection in order to develop the social, emotional, and cultural lens and competencies occurs during the field experience. Essentially, what starts in the coursework—understanding the anchor competencies; learning what it looks like to teach with a social,

TABLE 4.1 University of Dayton anchor competencies program matrix for Department of Teacher Education: Adolescence to Young Adult Program Grades 7-12

	DEVELOP SOCIAL, EMOTIONAL, AND CULTURAL "LENS"	BUILD TRUSTING RELATIONSHIPS	FOSTER SELF-REFLECTION	FOSTER GROWTH MINDSET	CULTIVATE PERSEVERANCE	CREATE CLASSROOM COMMUNITY	PROMOTE COLLABORATIVE LEARNING	RESPOND CONSTRUCTIVELY ACROSS DIFFERENCES
Explore Assumptions	EDT 338: Teaching, Learning and Management/ Lab	EDT 431, 432, 433, 434, 435: Content Methods	EDT 338: Teaching, Learning and Management/ Lab EDT 481: Adolescence to Young Adult Assessment	EDT 481: Adolescence to Young Adult Assessment EDT 431, 432, 433, 434, 435: Content Methods edTPA	EDT 431, 432, 433, 434, 435: Content Methods	EDT 431, 432, 433, 434, 435: Content Methods	EDT: Content Methods EDT 436 AYA Capstone Seminar Student Teaching
Model	EDT 338: Teaching, Learning and Management/ Lab	EDT 481: Adolescence to Young Adult Assessment Student Teaching	EDT 338: Teaching, Learning and Management/ Lab EDT 481: Adolescence to Young Adult Assessment	EDT 481: Adolescence to Young Adult Assessment EDT 431, 432, 433, 434, 435: Content Methods edTPA	EDT 431, 432, 433, 434, 435: Content Methods	EDT 459: Critical Reading and Writing in the Content Area EDT 431, 432, 433, 434, 435: Content Methods	EDT: Content Methods EDT 436 AYA Capstone Seminar Student Teaching
Provide Practice	EDT 338: Teaching, Learning and Management/ Lab	EDT 481: Adolescence to Young Adult Assessment Student Teaching	EDT 338: Teaching, Learning and Management/ Lab EDT 481: Adolescence to Young Adult Assessment	EDT 481: Adolescence to Young Adult Assessment EDT 431, 432, 433, 434, 435: Content Methods edTPA	EDT 431, 432, 433, 434, 435: Content Methods	EDT 459: Critical Reading and Writing in the Content Area EDT 431, 432, 433, 434, 435: Content Methods	EDT 431, 432, 433, 434, 435: Content Methods EDT 436 AYA Capstone Seminar Student Teaching
Provide Opportunity for Reflection	EDT 338: Teaching, Learning and Management/ Lab	EDT 481: Adolescence to Young Adult Assessment Student Teaching	EDT 338: Teaching, Learning and Management/ Lab EDT 481: Adolescence to Young Adult Assessment	EDT 481: Adolescence to Young Adult Assessment EDT 431, 432, 433, 434, 435: Content Methods edTPA	EDT 431, 432, 433, 434, 435: Content Methods	EDT 431, 432, 433, 434, 435: Content Methods	EDT 431, 432, 433, 434, 435: Content Methods EDT 436 AYA Capstone Seminar Student Teaching

emotional, and cultural lens; and exploring one's assumptions and beliefs that will affect decision-making as a teacher—continues, expands, and intensifies during the field experience. Interestingly, there is significant research that says that the field experience is the most important and influential part of the program.[24]

The field experience generally involves three parts and the participation of two professionals, making it even more complicated than the university courses. The three parts include: (1) the actual time that the candidate spends planning lessons, observing, teaching, and receiving coaching from their cooperating teacher; (2) the field seminars which the university supervisors hold with their students; and (3) the observations of the candidates conducted by the supervisors and cooperating teachers. The number of times seminars are held varies across programs, as do the number of times that supervisors and cooperating teachers conduct classroom observations. To add to the complexity, university supervisors are often adjunct rather than full-time faculty and are not required to attend faculty meetings. In fact, in many programs, there is insufficient funding to pay either the supervisors or the cooperating teachers to attend professional development sessions either at the university or at a school site. This leads to fragmentation between what the candidates are learning at the university and what they see modeled in the field.

Building the social, emotional, and cultural lens during coursework begins but by no means ends with introducing candidates to the concepts of the anchor competencies framework. Just as we discourage social, emotional, and cultural competencies from being a series of brief lessons for students, we discourage this approach with teacher candidates. Faculty should certainly devote class time to explaining and examining the competencies, but this must be followed up, reinforced, and deepened by rich classroom learning experiences during student teaching. The lens has to be modeled by faculty, explored through ongoing and in-depth conversations, and practiced on a regular basis with ample opportunity for discussion and reflection.

Field seminars

Seminars are a good opportunity to apply the whole framework because they are not driven by a single topic. University supervisors can support the continuous use of the social, emotional, and cultural lens to inform practice by providing a variety of opportunities at seminars. During these sessions, as in the course seminars, supervisors can use cooperatively structured activities and provide activities to build class community. For example, the supervisor might start the first session with the commonly used "What's in a name?" activity, where candidates first write down the answer to the following questions:

- Choosing one of your names, what do you know about how that name was chosen?
- Does that name have a meaning that you would be willing to share?
- What do you like about your name, if anything?
- What don't you like about your name, if anything?
- What do you like to be called?

The supervisor can then note that they have been practicing using the anchor competencies of building trusting relationships by building rapport and creating community by fostering individual voice. Hopefully, the anchors have been used across courses so the reference to these competencies is a source of programmatic consistency. The supervisor can then explore with the candidates their expectations for what they will learn in their field experience as well as what they are concerned about related to their students and their cooperating teachers. She can then ask them whether it was helpful to share, and how these activities have hopefully decreased their stress level. Often, candidates have discovered that others have similar concerns and that they are all in it together and will support one another. Finally, the supervisor can point out that what she is doing with them—giving them a chance to share their feelings and concerns and beginning to develop trust as a learning community—is exactly what they can do in their classrooms!

As the semester progresses, supervisors can provide opportunities at seminars either online or in person for candidates to view videos of teaching practice and analyze these videos. In a seminar discussion, candidates can hone their use of the lens by identifying which anchor competencies are present and what the teacher did (or should have done) at the beginning of the year for the students to begin development of the social, emotional, and cultural competencies. Starting with the use of videos of other teachers lowers the stress of the candidates, allowing them to really analyze the lesson. After they have built trust within their group, worked on a growth mindset, and created community, they will be ready to share and analyze their own videos together, developing these social, emotional, and cultural competencies as well as those of self-reflection, perseverance, and responding constructively across differences. If the supervisor explicitly refers to these competencies and how they are being modeled in the seminar, the candidates receive further reinforcement about how the anchors are integrated into teaching practice rather than becoming an add-on.

Another useful activity that can help candidates analyze their own assumptions and beliefs as well as work with the anchor competencies is to have candidates read and analyze a written teaching case. As with the videos, we recommend starting with third-person vignettes to keep the stress level low so that candidates can concentrate on developing the lens. Later they can bring written vignettes from their field experience to analyze in small or whole groups, again analyzing these real-life classroom experiences using the Anchor Competencies Framework. An example of a teaching case that provides a rich opportunity for discussion of one's assumptions and beliefs about homework practices concerns a high school student named Vanessa, who did not turn in her homework paper to the history teacher on time:

> On Wednesday morning, Vanessa frantically asked her English teacher, Ms. Krauss, if she could use the classroom computer to type and print out a history paper she was supposed to hand in on Tuesday. When Ms. Krauss asked her why she was late with the work, she explained that the computer she had at home was not working, and that she couldn't go over to anyone else's house to work on it because she had to stay home to babysit her little brother until her mom got home from work at 11:00 p.m. The student was extremely upset because her history teacher had said that papers turned in late would be downgraded a full letter grade.
>
> Ms. Krauss decided to discuss the situation with her colleague, Mr. Cantrell, Vanessa's history teacher. She told him the student's story, assuming

that he would then discuss it with the student directly and figure out something that would be fair. Instead, Mr. Cantrell told Ms. Krauss that his expectations regarding homework were rigorous and that he didn't make exceptions, and that Vanessa needed to learn to accept consequences. He further said that he thought Ms. Krauss was "way too easy" in her thinking.

Some questions about this vignette to get the discussion started with student teachers could include:

- What assumptions does each teacher make about the goals of homework?
- What might you do if you were the history teacher in this situation and why?
- What anchor competencies are, or should be, attended to in this situation?

After discussing this case, many teacher candidates pointed out that Mr. Cantrell needed to explore his assumptions: why he gives homework, and its purpose in supporting student learning. Is it to give them practice in the workplace responsibility of meeting a deadline? Is it to provide them with independent practice related to an academic standard of summarizing research on a topic and writing a coherent essay about what they found?

The candidates discussed what they might do in this situation, considering the anchor competencies. The candidates realized that no matter which goal Mr. Cantrell focused on, or even if he was addressing both goals, he had not done the essential work of building a trusting relationship with his students, which, in turn, led to a missed opportunity for learning. If Vanessa had felt comfortable talking to Mr. Cantrell when she had a problem, and if he had made clear to the students at the beginning of the year that he was there to support them, then she would more likely have gone to him with her dilemma. He would then have had the opportunity to help her problem-solve about what to do, so that rather than getting upset and grasping at straws, she would have been able to recognize and manage her emotions (self-reflection) and therefore, develop helpful strategies to cultivate perseverance by setting and monitoring her goals. As the reader can see, this analysis requires a completely different way of thinking about classroom practice than is often used.

Another written teaching case we have used with teaching candidates models positive ways of using the anchor competencies. It describes Shaneen, an African American sixth-grade student:

> During the first lesson after lunch time, Leann, the teacher, has asked the students to get into their teams of four to do a social studies activity using reference books from the library to look up facts about their chosen wild animal. Leann goes over to the group that includes Shaneen, observing that there is an issue. Shaneen is completely disengaged from her group. She sits wearing her coat, with her hood over her head, and her arms are crossed. The teacher sees that the other students are frustrated that Shaneen is not participating. Leann asks if Shaneen can come help her retrieve some additional resources for the group. During their time doing this task, the teacher asks Shaneen about lunchtime. Shaneen begins to talk about how two of her friends shut her out of a game of tetherball. She is angry and hurt. Leann acknowledged how that must have hurt Shaneen and said they should spend some time at the end of the day discussing how she could handle it. Leann then identified the skills that Shaneen brought to the group work that they really needed for the current activity. She was great at writing and bringing together different ideas generated by her group. Leann suggested that Shaneen go back to the group and help them, and that later that day they would problem-solve about the lunchtime episode. Shaneen agreed, took off her coat, brought over some books, and began working with her team.

In the above case, it is the individual context, more than anything, that is influencing the student's ability to engage academically. She has come in from lunch with her stress level high, making it physiologically difficult for her to concentrate and use her brain. If Leann had assumed that Shaneen was trying to be obstinate and confrontational with her, she might have told Shaneen to leave the group for time out, or taken points off her behavior chart. No learning would have occurred. Instead, Leann paid attention to the individual context that Shaneen was bringing to the class after lunch, and she addressed how that was inhibiting her ability to work. By Leann responding to the situation the way she did, Shaneen got practice in how to talk about what was really bothering her, engaging in self-reflection, and developing her ability to persevere. Additionally, Leann was articulating an affirming counternarrative to Shaneen about her capabilities.

In addition to case studies, course faculty and university supervisors can encourage candidates to share lesson plans they have developed. These can be analyzed in terms of the extent to which any of the anchor competencies are present in the lesson, or how they could integrate certain ones more than they have. The university supervisors can also share videos of lessons for the candidates to analyze using the framework to guide their analysis. As they feel more secure, candidates can then bring in videos of lessons they have implemented for analysis and reflection with their peers. Finally, candidates can bring to a seminar student work samples of one student having a difficult time in a subject area, and brainstorm in small groups the challenges with certain anchor competencies that might contribute to that student's struggles. They could then use the framework to generate ideas to take back to their classroom.

Putting the Pieces Together

As we have said earlier, many of these teaching strategies are things that teachers are already doing and that teachers-in-training are learning to use, thanks to preparation programs and thoughtful faculty. It is not uncommon now for teachers to be working toward using cooperative learning, providing asset-based feedback, and encouraging a growth mindset. But the Anchor Competencies Framework can help bring these pieces together as part of a cohesive approach, and it provides a process for developing them thoroughly by exploring assumptions and beliefs, modeling, practice, and reflection, so that they are not implemented in a "drive-by" approach in classrooms.

For this to work, the reality is that everyone involved in preparing teachers must engage in some difficult and emotional work. This includes examining our beliefs about how both children and adults learn and what they are capable of, and being willing to reevaluate those beliefs in the face of conflicting evidence or perspectives. It is essential to provide an environment that is safe so that everyone—those who prepare candidates and the candidates themselves—can take risks, persevere, and change. In such an environment, everyone can acknowledge their missteps and the need for improvement without feeling distraught or fearing punishment. As Suzanne heard one school administrator put it, "What we learn today doesn't make what we did yesterday wrong; it makes what we do tomorrow better." That's an important perspective to embrace in doing the work of teaching with a social, emotional, and cultural lens, because no one can become an expert overnight or even in one year, no matter how strong the teacher preparation program is. This work takes ongoing learning and growth, which can be encouraged by the next stage of the teacher pipeline—professional development, which is the focus of our next chapter.

CHAPTER 5

Incorporating the Framework in Schools

PROFESSIONAL DEVELOPMENT NEEDS and teacher growth do not end after teachers receive their credentials. In order for the social, emotional, and cultural lens to become firmly part of instruction, teachers need continuing support with opportunities to explore their assumptions and beliefs, view powerful modeling by other teachers, and practice and reflect as they build the social, emotional, and cultural competencies. Too often, the fundamental work of weaving together academic learning with social, emotional, and cultural competencies is left to those who have a special interest in it—those who opt in to professional development opportunities on how to lead restorative justice circles or who attend mindfulness practice with other educators. While teachers who are passionate about these issues should indeed have development and leadership opportunities, the problem with placing all of the responsibility on them is that students are affected by their relationships with *every* educator. Students learn from the habits and behaviors modeled by their math teachers. They either get or miss opportunities to learn about navigating conflicts in gym class. The way their English teachers talk about people from other cultures burrows deeply and often subconsciously into their minds.

By using the Anchor Competencies Framework, school leaders, teachers, and other staff can not only weave the competencies into everyday instructional interactions, they can also create coherence among the many promising but disjointed efforts that exist in schools today, like SEL curricula and character education programs, whole-school behavior management programs like Positive Behavior Interventions and Supports (PBIS), Multitiered Systems of Support (MTSS), and initiatives focused on suicide prevention, bullying, violence, trauma, and other mental health issues facing our schools. All of these efforts have value, but many schools are struggling to make sense of how they fit together and how to make social, emotional, and cultural learning an ongoing and meaningful part of schools. The Anchor Competencies Framework can provide a way to connect those pieces by ensuring that the core competencies are modeled, practiced, and reinforced throughout all of those initiatives and throughout the school day and year. Whether a student is receiving Tier 3 supports for mental health concerns or not, whether a teacher is actively working to prevent bullying or not, the fundamental competencies that all adults and students need to address these problems will be built. And it will not be left to chance or random assignment of students to classrooms to determine which students get social, emotional, and culturally competent teachers and which do not. This chapter describes how the framework can be used in professional development with teachers in the field.

PROFESSIONAL DEVELOPMENT STRUCTURES

There are many effective professional development methods and approaches used in schools today, but many others that do not meet the core criteria of quality. Professional development should be sustained, job-embedded, collaborative, and data-driven.[1] Nonevaluative coaching, professional development communities, networked improvement communities, and other approaches meet these criteria (when done well). The traditional "one-shot" workshop does not meet them, especially for a topic as complex as social, emotional, and cultural competence that requires deep reflection and consistent practice.

Many schools and districts already have high-quality professional development structures in place, into which the social, emotional, and cultural anchor competencies can be embedded. For example, instructional coaches who observe and provide feedback to teachers on a regular basis are well positioned to support teachers to incorporate the anchor competencies in their instructional planning, implementation, and reflection. (The observation protocol we described in chapter 3 can be useful for this purpose. Templates are provided in appendixes B and C.) Thanks in part to CASEL's Collaborating Districts Initiative (CDI), which has provided support in incorporating social and emotional learning in districts around the country since 2011, a number of school systems, including Austin, Texas, have begun to incorporate SEL into their coaching processes.[2] Districts like Anchorage, Alaska; Atlanta, Georgia; and the North East Independent School District of San Antonio, Texas, employ SEL specialists who work across schools to support implementation; assess resources and needs; and support classroom, school, and community programming; as well as establish systems for continuous improvement.[3] The Anchor Competencies Framework could be useful to these districts as well as any others moving to bring social, emotional, and cultural practices to school sites. The framework can provide the focus for integration of these practices across the preK–12 curriculum and support districts in bringing together attention to social and emotional learning skills with culturally responsive teaching practices. It is important to ensure, however, that the framework does not get sidelined by being used only by a district's SEL department or its chief equity officer, but instead should be understood and infused across all district professional development efforts.

AN UNDERUTILIZED APPROACH: UNIVERSITY-DISTRICT PARTNERSHIPS

University-district partnerships are a promising but underutilized approach to professional development in social, emotional, and cultural competencies. Districts can take advantage of the knowledge and resources of experts in psychology, ethnic and cultural studies, educational leadership, and other areas at the university. Districts that provide field placements for teacher candidates in university preservice programs have a particularly efficient and effective way to leverage university partnerships. In such districts, cooperating teachers who mentor and oversee teacher candidates can play an important role in their development, including whether and how they think about growing the social, emotional, and cultural competencies of both themselves and their students. Yet, too often, this opportunity is missed. Even worse, a lack of intentionality in selecting and training cooperating teachers can lead to poor modeling of the competencies and failure of teacher candidates to develop the skills and habits of supporting students effectively.

University teacher education programs have not only an opportunity but a responsibility to change this situation by building cooperating teachers' social, emotional, and cultural competence through university-district professional development collaboration. These partnerships benefit everyone. University programs benefit by graduating more effective teachers, who in turn support students to be successful. Districts' cooperating teachers benefit because they develop new knowledge and skills and, often, leadership capacity that helps them stay engaged and advance in their careers. Schools benefit because teachers they have already hired become more effective and often become the seeds of change for a more widespread shift in culture and instructional practice. Furthermore, they help to create a pipeline of new teachers who are well prepared and ready to be effective in district classrooms once they graduate. It's a win all around, with real potential for systemic, lasting change if universities and districts work together toward the same goal of integrating social, emotional, and cultural competencies within both educational settings across the professional development pipeline.

The Unique Role of Cooperating Teachers

As we said above, school district cooperating teachers play an important and lasting role in the careers of teachers-in-training. They play a key role in what teacher candidates learn to do in classrooms and how they think about teaching. In most programs, candidates will work in the classroom of no more than two teachers. As such, these cooperating teachers need to be strong exemplars and models, and they should be familiar with and supportive of the language, values, and practices provided in the university coursework. Yet there is typically little or no application process or specific criteria for district and school leaders in selecting cooperating teachers. They are chosen based on decisions by the school principal and need only to have at least three years of teaching experience. For the principal, logistical needs can preempt choosing teachers for their advanced pedagogical and coaching skills.[4] Contrast this with other fields like medicine, where chief residents who mentor junior residents go through a rigorous selection process and hold a status of high honor. Thus, a teacher may be selected because she has an upcoming parental leave and the principal sees the opportunity for the teacher candidate to become an easy replacement during her absence. In other cases we have seen candidates placed in classrooms where there are many behavior challenges and teachers could use "another pair of hands," as some have put it—not an ideal situation for a teacher just starting out.

Cooperating teachers typically receive little or no training to do this job, nor adequate time or compensation. When it comes to modeling the social, emotional, and cultural lens, few cooperating teachers are well prepared because neither their teacher education programs nor their schools have focused on building these capacities. In most cases, it is therefore a game of chance whether a teacher candidate will be mentored by a teacher who creates community in his classroom and responds constructively across differences when faced with conflicts across race and class, or by one who believes these skills are not part of her job, that behavior challenges should be dealt with strictly by sending students to the principal, or that being "color blind" is the best way to approach racial and cultural differences.

Given this reality in schools, teacher education programs need to play a role in cultivating the social, emotional, and cultural lens among cooperating teachers. Of course, this must be done in partnership with districts and schools, which means that programs should be intentional about the districts with whom they work and where they assign teacher candidates. As partners, there should be an advisory university-district group that *together* designs criteria for selection of cooperating teachers and the support they will receive in that role. In one California district that has worked closely with the Center for Reaching & Teaching the Whole Child and its university partner, San José State University, such a relationship has built the district's capacity to the point that its leaders and teachers can carry on this work largely on their own. It is our vision, and our sincere hope, that a generation from now, the social, emotional, and cultural lens will be established enough in both teacher preparation programs and schools that intensive investments in training will be less necessary because both universities and districts will be committed to the lens, and cooperating teachers will be using it as a matter of course. In the meantime, however, these investments and strong partnerships between universities and districts are vital.

Cultivating the Competencies in Cooperating Teachers: The Case of Sunnyvale School District

As a result of the establishment of CRTWC around 2008, when Nancy was a professor at SJSU, the university's K–8 teacher education department made a strong commitment to cultivating social, emotional, and cultural competencies in future teachers. The faculty efforts to integrate these competencies in the content of the university coursework clearly were documented in the syllabi participating professors had created. However, we needed to know if the candidates agreed that professors were actually teaching what they thought they were teaching. So in 2014 we hired WestEd, a nonpartisan, nonprofit, research, development, and service agency, to evaluate our efforts. Their findings indicated that although CRTWC's work with university teacher educators made an impact on faculty, supervisors, and candidates, candidates needed more opportunities to practice these competencies in the field.[5] We realized we needed to address a missing link and work more closely with the districts where students were placed for fieldwork and, more specifically, with the cooperating teachers.

For many years, we had been placing several of our teacher candidates in the Sunnyvale School District (SSD) for their field placement experiences. SSD is a medium-sized district in the San Francisco Bay area that serves an ethnically and socioeconomically diverse student population. At three of the eight elementary schools, a majority of students receive free or reduced price lunch, and approximately 31 percent of district students are English language learners, many of whom were born in Mexico, Central America, or South America. Social, emotional, and cultural competence is important in all schools, but several factors sharpened the need for this in Sunnyvale. The homeless population is large enough that one principal organized a visit for her faculty to a local shelter so that they could see firsthand the context in which their students were living outside the classroom. A large number of immigrant families, some undocumented, were experiencing anxiety over changing immigration policies and growing anti-immigrant sentiment in the US. Even among many affluent families in the district, the job pressures of the fast-paced, transient Silicon Valley environment placed unusual stresses on families.

Through our partnership with a nonprofit organization, Acknowledge Alliance, which was also working with SSD, we discovered that the deputy superintendent of human resources, Dr. Michael Gallagher, had made a commitment to bringing social and emotional learning practices to the district after conducting research on the topic during his doctoral program. This helped to make SSD an ideal district with which to start a deeper partnership, cultivating it as a "lab district" for developing and honing strategies to incorporate the Anchor Competencies Framework.

As a starting point, CRTWC, while still an Organizational Research Unit within SJSU Lurie College of Education, proposed to provide a series of four two-hour professional development sessions for cooperating teachers on social, emotional, and cultural competencies. CRTWC staff conducted the sessions with cooperating teachers at a school site during the school day, to show that we valued their time and did not want to overburden them or want them to view this as an add-on to their existing responsibilities. During the sessions, teacher candidates assumed responsibility for the cooperating teachers' classrooms, receiving a half day of substitute pay for doing so. This structure gave them the opportunity to practice solo teaching while their cooperating teachers received the gift of time to think, discuss, and learn with colleagues. The district, recognizing the importance of the social, emotional, and cultural work, agreed to provide a substitute teacher in the cases where a student teacher was not available.

Using the Anchor Competencies Framework as the foundation, the goals of the program were for cooperating teachers to understand and use a common language about teaching with a social, emotional, and cultural perspective; develop the ability to integrate the anchor competencies into their own teaching practice; and develop the ability to coach teacher candidates to integrate the competencies into their work with students. More specifically, we expected cooperating teachers who completed the program to be able to:

- Explain the connection between social, emotional, and cultural competencies for teachers and learners and student achievement, using a common language
- Model lessons and practices grounded in the anchors framework to build a safe physical, social-emotional, and intellectual learning environment
- Identify students' social and emotional skills needed within content-specific lessons and the anchor competencies and potential teacher moves to develop them
- Use coteaching strategies to model the anchor competencies for their teacher candidates and provide the candidates with extensive opportunities to practice and reflect on the development of the social, emotional, and cultural competencies in themselves and with their students

During the sessions, we used videos, written teaching cases, and practice activities for cooperating teachers to analyze how the competencies could be used and to give them practice using them in their own teaching and mentoring of candidates. Some of the videos were created by CRTWC—for example, a faculty member modeling how to incorporate the lens into math instruction—while others were already available online. During one session, for instance, we focused on the technique of giving formative feedback to build the growth mindset anchor. The cooperating teachers viewed a video of a SJSU professor providing information on what constitutes effective formative feedback and modeling its use with the candidates in her seminar. For "homework" before the next session, the cooperative teachers were to ask their teacher candidates to observe them and write down verbatim formative feedback the cooperating teacher provided to the students during a given lesson. This activity provided modeling for the candidate, fostered self-reflection and reflective listening by the cooperating teacher, and supported both the cooperating teacher and candidate in building a trusting relationship. These anchor competencies were used in the service of improving the practice of both the cooperating teacher and candidate.

Throughout the sessions, it was important to us that cooperating teachers not perceive the work as yet another add-on to their already extensive responsibilities. Additionally, we wanted to be sure that they saw that the Common Core State Standards competencies were dependent on attention to the social, emotional, and cultural competencies on which we were focusing. We also wanted to convey the message that working on social, emotional, and cultural competencies has to happen as a parallel process at all levels of the system; we were going to pay attention to the teachers' own skills and needs just as we expected them to pay attention to students' skills and needs.

For example, we knew we needed to take into account the context that cooperating teachers brought with them and how it would influence their ability to focus during the sessions, just like the framework encourages teachers to pay attention to their students' moods, emotional needs, and life situations. The cooperating teachers usually arrived at our meetings after stopping by their classrooms to greet their students and make sure their teacher candidates had everything they needed to teach that morning. In other words, the cooperating teachers did not come in as blank slates. Some of them, no doubt, had dealt with a concerned parent, had rushed to get their own children to school before going to work, or had not slept well the night before.

To provide the consistency and modeling that we see as so important in this work, we began each session with a centering activity, one that teachers could in turn use with their own students. We not only modeled these activities with the cooperating teachers, but gave them descriptions of the activities as handouts so that they could then practice using them in their own classrooms. At the next session we would then ask who had tried the activity in their class and reflect on how it went.

At the first session we started by doing a three-minute mindfulness activity, a breathing and visualization exercise to help them focus on the present moment. At the conclusion of that activity, we asked them to imagine a shopping bag by their chair, to make an imaginary list in their heads of all their "to do" items for that day, and then put that list in the bag and put the imaginary bag under their chair. We told them the bag would be waiting for them when they left the session but that for now, they could put it aside. After a few more deep breaths, we asked them to open their eyes or look up. We could sense a palpable downward shift in the level of nervous, unfocused energy emanating from the group. We were ready to begin. After talking about CRTWC's work, the importance of the parallel process of addressing both teachers' and students' social, emotional, and cultural competencies, and a general overview of the goals of this professional development experience, we shared a slide that said:

Teaching can be intense and exhausting . . .

"There is research on the extraordinary number of decisions that a teacher has to make at any given moment—more decisions minute-by-minute than a brain surgeon. The most conservative estimate from this data has teachers making approximately 130 decisions per hour during a six-hour school day, and this reflects only those decisions made within the classroom."[6]

There were visible nods of agreement and a few long sighs emanating from the group. We reiterated that in order for teachers to support children, teachers need support, too.

To further emphasize what we meant, we next engaged the teachers in an exercise called the Resilient Garden (adapted from Growing a Garden by Melanie Miller [see sidebar]).[7] In this activity, cooperating teachers were asked to identify those people who support them in their professional lives, what activities they did to take care of themselves, and what things got in the way of their success as a teacher and their vision of themselves as highly competent educators. In doing this activity, many of them realized that they did not sufficiently take care of themselves, making it even more difficult to overcome the steep barriers all teachers face to becoming highly competent. By applying the anchor competencies directly to these veteran teachers' own professional lives, we connected with them at a deep level and showed them the value of our approach.

Each of the subsequent three sessions, typically spaced about a month apart, were divided into two parts. First, participants shared what they had implemented, thought about, and worked on with their teacher candidates related to the anchor competencies. In other words, they talked about the modeling, practice, and reflection that had occurred, together with the associated challenges and triumphs. The second part of each session provided opportunities to watch a video or analyze a written case study of classroom practice

THE RESILIENT GARDEN

(adapted from "Growing a Garden" by Melanie Miller)

Instructions to participants:

1. Take out a piece of blank paper and a pencil or pen.

2. Draw a circle that will be the center of a flower (about 1/3 from the top of the paper). Put your name in the circle. Give your flower seven petals. Think about a time with one of your students when you felt really connected and were being the kind of teacher you want to be. Think of words that describe you in that time. Put one word or adjective in each petal. Take note if you are struggling to fill in all seven petals.

3. Every flower needs stems and leaves. Give your flower a stem and four leaves. In each leaf put the name of a person who supports you as a teacher. Take note if you are struggling to fill all four leaves.

4. Every plant needs roots so give your plant ten roots. On each root write something you do for fun. Take note if you are struggling to fill in all ten roots.

5. Every garden has weeds. Draw four weeds. On your weeds, write something that you do that gets in the way of you being the teacher you want to be.

6. Lastly, make a butterfly flying by the flower. Write a hope for yourself as a teacher or a small step toward becoming more of the teacher you want to be.

Explanation of the garden:

Petals are our need to feel capable and connected as a teacher; if we aren't feeling capable and connected, we cannot flower.

Leaves are the support systems that make us feel love and belonging. The flower cannot thrive without leaves.

Roots are how we take care of ourselves. We need the roots to nourish the flower.

Weeds are the parts of our characters that get in the way of making more flowers. These are the attributes we have that do not serve us well.

Butterfly represents the possibility of what we can be and where we can go. A butterfly emerges from the chrysalis and spreads its wings to soar. It represents the courage and hope to move forward.

(This exercise can be modified for use with students and parents.)

using their social, emotional, and cultural lens so that they could be more and more comfortable with the anchor competencies in practice.

The data we gathered on the impact of these professional development sessions indicated that the cooperating teachers renewed their excitement about teaching. Comments indicated that they relished being provided a common language for discussion of social, emotional, and cultural competencies to analyze their practice as well as specific anchors and accompanying moves to integrate the social, emotional, and cultural competencies in their work with children. These teachers routinely indicated that their work with CRTWC was helping them do what makes them feel best—teaching to the whole child and helping their colleagues do the same. As one teacher said, "I've taught in the Sunnyvale School District (SSD) for eleven years, and I think it's the most important professional development I've participated in. I cannot overstate how important it is for teachers to develop their social, emotional, and cultural lens and to keep working and engaging with the ideas. I think I was a reasonable teacher before, but I know I am a better teacher now. I am more compassionate and better able to think long-term rather than just reacting to challenges in the moment. My lessons are more effective and I've seen greater gains in student achievement."

Other comments by SSD cooperating teachers included:

"We need as teachers to foster SEL everyday as part as our routine and goals."

"Be intentional; student-focused; structure lessons [to] integrate with SEL strategies. What teachers say to students and how they [say it] has a major impact on student perception[s]."

"I need to be more aware of how my language affects students and their own self-esteem. [I need to establish] a growth vs. fixed mindset in my class."

"I need to focus and verbalize more with the class [on] emotions and feelings. We need as teachers to foster [anchor competencies] every day as part of our routine and goals. [I recognized the] importance of developing relationships/trust in classroom—importance of teaching conversation—reminder that we are teaching SEL everyday."

Seeds of Change

It was clear to us that this professional development on the anchor competencies for cooperating teachers was having an impact on their teaching, and they loved being part of a university-district professional development community. But more than that was happening—we were developing teacher leaders as "seeds of change" who were sharing what they were learning from us with their school site administrators and colleagues. Further, we were building a pipeline of highly qualified new teachers who would soon be looking for jobs, and who were already prepared to fulfill the district's commitment to applying the social, emotional, and cultural lens in teaching.

As seeds of change, the cooperating teachers were helping to move the district toward increasing institutionalization of social, emotional, and cultural competencies as an expected goal. Many cooperating teachers who participated have subsequently taken on leadership roles, such as instructional coach and district SEL director, in which they are able to spread their knowledge about and commitment to the social, emotional, and cultural lens. This kind of leadership development is beneficial in many ways. Research shows that teachers have longer and more successful careers in education when they have opportunities for leadership, such as coaching or department leadership.[8] Although we do not have quantitative data on the long-term retention of cooperating teachers who participated in the CRTWC professional development, we do have qualitative data documenting multiple examples of teachers who deepened their professional commitment for years to come. Consider the following examples.

Barbara Papamarcos, a cooperating teacher who participated in one of the first cohorts and now teaches in Wisconsin's Port Washington–Saukville School District, found that it reignited her passion for teaching and reconnected her with her purpose. She decided to make social, emotional, and cultural practices her professional goal for the year while still in Sunnyvale School District and shared what she was doing with her principal. Noting Barbara's enthusiasm, the principal asked her to share some of her learning during a staff meeting with her grade-level team and then to lead an hour-long staff development session about social, emotional, and cultural competencies with the whole school faculty. This session, in turn, led to the principal supporting additional school site efforts to bring social, emotional, and cultural competence into the classrooms of other teachers. Papamarcos continued in her role in SSD for several years before relocating to Wisconsin. She recently emailed CRTWC leaders with the following comments:

I want to share the impact you have had on my teaching and how it is still driving my instruction today. The training you provided me in Sunnyvale and the opportunities that you offered catapulted my teaching to a new level. This year I attached my professional goals for the year to [an assessment of students' social and emotional skills and strategies]. It is transforming my goals as a teacher. I had my students create their own social emotional folders and keep track of their own practices and how those practices help them to perform academically. It is so individual which strategies support each learner and me!

I am at a place where I can say to my students, "I need this strategy for me right now." And . . . amazingly, they give me the 5 minutes or whatever. On top of that, they do the strategies/activities with me and I am finding a new level of academic concentration. It isn't every moment but when the moment counts—we can dial in quickly. This year before testing we did a lot of guided imagery and it was impressive how the kids used it to support their own learning.

When I shared my goal with my administrator, at first it was questioned: why would I pick a "soft skill" focus rather than an academic quantitative goal focus? I shared my idea that if the SEL pieces are in place then the academics will grow . . . After my recent goal conference, my administrator asked if I would be willing to share my results with the staff. In addition, I am bringing strategies to my team meeting each week that we practice and then I encourage them to use it in their own classroom.

Rachel Bacosa, a first-grade teacher in SSD, who had attended four years of sessions with us, was also asked to lead professional development for the faculty in her school and, after two years, was promoted to a new full-time position as district SEL coach. Rachel has therefore been able to cultivate the social, emotional, and cultural lens at many levels: with her students, her immediate colleagues, and the district. It has also deepened her own commitment to her career and the district and provided a stable leader for the district. Furthermore, seeing her take on the district role has provided a morale boost for veteran SSD teachers, who see that the district values both teaching experience and teachers' professional development efforts in its leadership.

These kinds of growth and positive outcomes have been possible because of some essential conditions, including a supportive school district; a strong university-district partnership; consistency in using the same social, emotional, and cultural language and approaches across university and district; a solid framework in which to ground the work; and that most essential but elusive element for schools: time. Dedicated time across an entire school year allowed ample opportunities for learning, practice, reflection, and improvement. Those processes are not only helpful for teachers, but are at the heart of the anchor competencies we want students to develop so that they can learn and thrive.

THE ROLE OF SCHOOL ADMINISTRATORS

Although partnerships with universities can be very beneficial, they are not necessary to incorporate the anchor competencies. This framework also provides site administrators within a district with a common language and the strategies they, too, need to use with their faculty. A full discussion of the role of school leaders is beyond the scope of this book, but it is worth mentioning that by using the framework, principals can begin to analyze their own practice, looking at how they structure and run faculty meetings, how coaches work with teachers, and how teachers are encouraged to work collaboratively. For example, principals can set the stage at the beginning of each year to create a safe and "brave space" where they engage the faculty in activities to build mutual trust and community.[9] Dr. Pam Cheng, principal at Lakewood Elementary School in SSD, was concerned that some of her teachers did not understand the circumstances their students were dealing with and were consequently not employing effective strategies to support them at school. In response, she used one faculty meeting to take her teachers on a field trip to the local homeless shelter, described earlier, as many of the children at this particular school lived there. For some of the teachers, the experience was not new, but for the majority of the staff, it was. Teachers came away with tears in their eyes. Cheng had used the experience to build knowledge about the conditions (or context, in the language of the framework) some of their students were living with, which might hamper their ability to complete their home-work. Cheng did not stop there. She then encouraged the teachers to practice reciprocal vulnerability, by talking together as a learning community about how the experience had impacted them and possibly changed their under-standing of their students. They discussed and shared strategies about what they would do differently to support but also challenge the students. These veteran teachers were thriving on the opportunity to extend their knowledge about their students and the strategies they could use to meet their needs. With the principal encouraging the faculty to try out new ideas, come to fac-ulty meetings to share what happened, and then be able to offer each other suggestions based on their experiences, she built a growth mindset among the teachers. Like their students, the faculty were being provided with the oppor-tunity to practice the anchor competencies among themselves and then were encouraged to reflect and integrate it within their teaching practice.

INFORMING DISTRICT POLICY

Although much of the work of developing social, emotional, and cultural com-petence must happen in schools and classrooms, policies and upper-level administration have an enormous influence on what goes on in those class-rooms. It can help or hinder efforts to do this work. Just as it can be used to inform teacher practices, the framework can inform the way administrators shape policies.

For example, American schools are beset by troubling racial disparities in disciplinary actions. Black students, especially boys and young men, are nearly three times more likely to be suspended and expelled than their White peers, even controlling for socioeconomic status, special education status, and gen-der.[10] Shockingly, these patterns start as early as preschool.[11] Scholars point to a number of disturbing reasons for these disparities, including implicit biases teachers hold against children of color.[12] Traditional methods of school disci-pline do not address these problems and can exacerbate the inequities.

To address these disparities, many districts are looking for alternatives to suspension, especially for nonviolent behavior.[13] Critics worry that revised discipline policies are letting students off the hook and failing to address problems.[14] This doesn't have to be the case, but district and school leaders need a solid understanding of student development and approaches to behavior in order to replace detrimental discipline policies with effective ones. The Anchor Competencies Framework can be the basis for reshaping these policies and, just as importantly, for preventing discipline problems in the first place.

The framework addresses racial bias by putting exploration of educators' assumptions and beliefs at the core of the work. It also grounds educators' approaches to behavior expectations and discipline in a philosophy of empathy and viewing each student as an individual. The more teachers seek to know and understand their students, the more they are able to pinpoint the underlying problems and help students address them, rather than applying an arbitrary punishment that may even reinforce the undesirable behavior. For example, as Nancy Rappaport and Jessica Minahan explain in their excellent and useful book *The Behavior Code*, if a student acts out to get attention or to get out of doing work that overwhelms him, sending him to the office won't help and will actually make him more likely to seek that reinforcement in the future.[15] Conversely, if a teacher comes to understand that a young child is physically aggressive because she likes the sensory stimulation, providing her an appropriate outlet will be far more effective—for her *and* her classmates—than repeatedly yelling at her, which will only serve to shame her and do nothing to reduce the behavioral need.

A social, emotional, and cultural lens on behavior is not a panacea, but it does open the door to more equitable and effective forms of discipline, like alternative disciplinary approaches such as restorative justice, or skill-building approaches like strategies to help students express their emotions constructively and manage anger. It also prepares educators to leverage approaches like PBIS and MTSS that aim to both prevent behavior problems and deal with them effectively when they occur.

SOCIAL AND EMOTIONAL LEARNING PROGRAMS

So far, we have said little about the role of curricular programs to teach SEL skills to students in today's schools. To be clear, we believe that these programs can be valuable for students, but that they are not sufficient on their own.

Curricular programs were the first approach chosen by early pioneers in this field in part because that is generally the way new skills and content are provided in our schools. They can be useful in spelling out the skills to be taught and providing the strategies a teacher can use to teach the skills. They also provide a sequence for skill development that can be very helpful to a teacher not familiar with SEL competencies. Curricular programs can help students focus, manage their emotions, work effectively with others, and set goals. This can empower students to take charge of their own needs and learning, and help them gradually learn to take care of these needs on their own, such as asking the teacher for a few minutes to calm down or visiting a calm-down corner as can be found in many classrooms.

Many of these programs have been researched for their effectiveness, and evaluations have provided evidence that programs that are high quality and implemented well promote better emotional classroom climates, higher connectedness between teachers and students, more support for student autonomy and leadership, better social relationships and emotional management, a greater focus on students' motivations and interests, and, in some cases, better academic achievement.[16] A meta-analysis of the impact of SEL programming indicated that programs were more likely to be effective when they embodied four characteristics captured in the acronym SAFE: Sequenced (activities and lessons were connected and coordinated so skills build on one another over time), Active (students were engaged in role plays, discussions, and other active forms of learning rather than listening to teacher lectures), Focused (the program had a clear emphasis on social and personal skills development, even if embedded in a more comprehensive school program), and Explicit (lessons clearly communicated to build specific skills).[17]

But relying solely on such programs has a number of limitations. By its very nature, a program becomes what teachers often call an "add-on"—one more topic of instruction that the teacher is supposed to address. Teachers may reasonably respond to such additions by saying, "I don't have the time to add anything else into the curriculum!" And practically speaking, new programs are usually costly. Schools and districts that receive foundation or government grants, or who are part of a short-term research project, may be able to initially support the cost of these programs, but what happens when the funding is gone and the teachers who were trained in the program have moved on? Indeed, in 2018 the charitable giving website DonorsChoose reported that "social and emotional learning" was one of the most frequently requested resources for which teachers asked members of the public to kick in funds.[18] Without adequate funding, SEL programs could go the way of other initially exciting curricular programs: sitting in the textbook room, gathering dust.

Furthermore, like any type of intervention, SEL programs are not universally effective, in large part because the quality of implementation varies greatly. Poor implementation of well-designed programs is linked with disappointing outcomes for students.[19] Incomplete or ineffective implementation can be due to many factors, including time constraints in school schedules, competing responsibilities, and lack of training and support. Further, even when they are implemented with fidelity, these programs rarely take the sociopolitical, cultural, and individual contexts of children, teachers, and schools into account. The assumption is that they will work effectively with diverse populations of children, but there has been little investigation into whether this assumption holds true.

Even the best program cannot improve students' skills if educators engage students in it for forty-five minutes a week and leave the concepts on the bookshelf the rest of the time, or if they isolate these competencies from the achievement of academic standards. And even the best teachers cannot achieve the potential of well-designed programs if they are not prepared with a solid foundation of the skills themselves. Investing in building teachers' understanding, knowledge, and capacity for modeling and encouraging social, emotional, and cultural competencies will certainly improve the chances that programs will be implemented fully, with fidelity, and in ways that value and are responsive to diverse children's cultures and life experiences. They may be more likely to provide a solid foundation in the concepts, rather than picking and choosing elements of the program without giving students the foundation or continuity they need, or making assumptions about children's understanding of social and emotional competencies without examining their own biases. Additionally, teachers who use a social, emotional, and cultural lens are likely to be more prepared to reinforce the skills taught in the program during teachable moments and everyday interactions with children, other school personnel, and caretakers.

It is important to note that we are not expecting teachers to be either therapists or mind readers; it would be counterproductive and nonsensical for teachers to ask every student about his feelings every day. Rather, we are saying that developing the lens enables a teacher to recognize the role of social and emotional needs and skills, ask the questions that will address the student's needs, and then create the space for a productive response. Often, that takes very little time or effort—but it does take awareness and intentionality.

GETTING CONNECTED

There is no one right or ideal way to develop a social, emotional, and cultural lens on teaching. Schools may partner with nonprofits or universities, hire consultants, or learn from available resources like this one and do the work of integrating them into their existing professional development structures and policies on their own. This work does not require outside personnel. It does, however, benefit from collaboration and support across levels. A teacher or team of teachers certainly can work on developing the lens on their own, and we encourage them to do so. But they will have more opportunities for learning and reinforcement if they are supported by a schoolwide or districtwide effort. And a principal's or instructional coach's work will be strengthened by policy and financial support. The good news is that this collaboration can go in both directions: individual educators and small-scale efforts can become the "existence proof" that this work is possible and beneficial, and the impetus for schools and districts to scale it. Scale is the topic of our next chapter, where we examine the roles that states, districts, and universities can play and how, in some cases, they are already doing it.

CHAPTER 6

Building the Bridge to Connect Theory and Practice

RECENTLY, NANCY TALKED with a professor in teacher education who works with large high-needs districts. After a conversation about his work with teacher candidates and teacher education faculty, he mused, "Are we ever going to have a time when children will want to come to school?" Nancy responded optimistically that all the work being done currently in the arenas of social and emotional learning and culturally responsive teaching practices will hopefully provide a positive response to his question. Educators are starting to see that work pay off. In a book by Curtis Linton and Bonnie Davis, Sandy Nobles, principal of J. Erik Jonsson Elementary School in Dallas, Texas, summed it up when she described the positive energy of a school with an equity culture where each person is valued and heard: "[It] feels so right when it works, and [school's] a great place to spend a day. You're with people that like the work they're doing. You're with children excited about coming to school and learning."[1]

But the truth is that in order for all schools to be great places, there needs to be a sea change. Educators need to get on the same page—across the continuum of professional development and across key agencies and organizations. Large-scale adoption by educators of social-emotional competencies and culturally responsive teaching practices requires coordinated leadership of districts, states, and universities in setting effective and consistent policies, performance expectations, and professional development.

Think back to the bridge between theory and practice that we asked you to imagine in chapter 1. If that bridge is going to be sturdy and able to promote a constant exchange between research-based knowledge and what we do with that knowledge in classrooms, we need to design a bridge in which all the parts fit together. That requires a common blueprint with shared assumptions. Otherwise, the bridge might serve as a connector for a few brave people willing to carefully climb from one side to the other, but it will not be useful for the masses.

In this chapter we will discuss the roles of three key entities—the state, the district, and the university—in constructing a sturdy bridge. Together, these entities can move forward with the work of reaching all students. The Anchor Competencies Framework can provide a guide to building a bridge that integrates social, emotional, and cultural practices throughout preK–12 curriculum and at all levels of professional development for teachers.

Research has helped us understand what it takes to scale this work.[2] In this chapter we identify an initial list of factors that need to be present at the state, district, and university levels, including: a roadmap that provides a common language and framework for the "on the ground" work; the support of high-level leadership; buy-in by the majority of staff and faculty; institutional and state-level policies and mandates that require integration of social, emotional, and cultural competencies in the work of educators; and committed resources, including dedicated time and funding, to support the work.

STATE LEVEL

States can play multiple roles in putting the Anchor Competencies Framework into practice. States set highly detailed standards for school curriculum, teacher credentialing, teacher training program accreditation, student discipline, and other aspects of schooling. Including standards focused on the anchor competencies can support the work of educational reform advocates to ensure that large-scale changes are made, and that they are consistent across districts and across different aspects of the education system. States also play a critical role by funding efforts that support the development of social, emotional, and cultural competencies. The following sections describe each of these essential roles.

Teacher Certification Standards

Teacher certification standards are used by teacher preparation programs and teacher educators to guide preservice training. Few states currently incorporate social and emotional learning competencies and culturally responsive teaching practices into their teacher performance standards. The Anchor Competencies Framework can help guide efforts to revise these standards, and then help teacher educators understand how to operationalize the standards. A promising outlier in teacher performance expectation trends is in California. The California Teacher Performance Expectations (2016) include attention to the role of social, emotional, and cultural competence in teaching and student outcomes.[3] But they do so in broad strokes only. For example, more specifics are needed to achieve the expectation of "positive interactions among students" embedded in a standard about creating and maintaining effective environments for student learning. Making these expectations really useful requires drilling down into what each of these standards looks like in practice. This is where the Anchor Competencies Framework can provide a common language and roadmap.

Below we provide four examples from the California State Teacher Performance Expectations (TPEs) and the anchors that map on to them. For each of the anchors, we provide related examples of teacher moves and supporting strategies. Table 6.1 shows how the TPEs and the anchor competencies are linked. They illustrate that the anchor competencies (and accompanying teacher moves and strategies) are not adding additional topics to cover in preservice training, but clarifying and operationalizing the existing required TPEs.

For example, fostering a growth mindset provides some direction about how to promote "productive student learning," and building trusting relationships and the specific teacher moves that accompany it in the framework is an important step in encouraging "positive interactions among students." The teacher moves and strategies we provide go further in explaining and providing examples to support the development of this and other competencies.

TABLE 6.1 TPE/anchor competencies/teacher moves connections

CALIFORNIA TEACHER PERFORMANCE EXPECTATIONS 2017	CORRESPONDING ANCHOR COMPETENCIES	TEACHER MOVES
TPE 1: Engaging and Supporting All Students in Learning Apply knowledge of students, including their prior experiences, interest, and social-emotional learning needs, as well as their funds of knowledge and cultural, language, and socioeconomic backgrounds, to engage them in learning.	Build trusting relationships	▪ Develop rapport ▪ Engage families ▪ Practice reciprocal vulnerability ▪ Employ trauma-informed practices
	Create classroom community	▪ Attend to status issues ▪ Foster individual voice ▪ Create a culture of engagement ▪ Affirm each other's assets
	Foster self-reflection	▪ Recognize and manage emotional reactions ▪ Examine biases ▪ Explore identity
	Cultivate perseverance	▪ Provide asset-based formative feedback ▪ Set and monitor goals ▪ Embrace productive struggles
TPE 2: Creating and Maintaining Effective Environments for Student Learning Promote students' social-emotional growth, development, and individual responsibility using positive interventions and supports, restorative justice, and conflict resolution practices to foster a caring community where each student is treated fairly and respectfully by adults and peers.	Build trusting relationships	▪ Develop rapport ▪ Engage families ▪ Practice reciprocal vulnerability ▪ Employ trauma-informed practices
	Respond constructively across differences	▪ Practice restorative justice ▪ Build capacity to make amends ▪ Identify and interrupt microaggressions
	Create classroom community	▪ Attend to status issues ▪ Foster individual voice ▪ Create a culture of engagement ▪ Affirm each other's assets

(continued)

TABLE 6.1 (CONTINUED) TPE/anchor competencies/teacher moves connections

CALIFORNIA TEACHER PERFORMANCE EXPECTATIONS 2017	CORRESPONDING ANCHOR COMPETENCIES	TEACHER MOVES
TPE 4: Planning Instruction and Designing Learning Experiences for All Students Plan, design, implement and monitor instruction … to provide access to the curriculum for all students by removing barriers … with developmentally, linguistically, and culturally appropriate learning activities, instructional materials, and resources for all students, including the full range of English learners.	Build trusting relationships	∎ Develop rapport ∎ Engage families ∎ Practice reciprocal vulnerability ∎ Employ trauma-informed practices
	Foster growth mindset	∎ Articulate affirming counternarratives ∎ Shift to positive self-talk ∎ Connect learning to the brain
	Cultivate perseverance	∎ Provide asset-based formative feedback ∎ Set and monitor goals ∎ Embrace productive struggles
	Create classroom community	∎ Attend to status issues ∎ Foster individual voice ∎ Create a culture of engagement ∎ Affirm each other's assets
	Respond constructively across differences	∎ Practice restorative justice ∎ Build capacity to make amends ∎ Identify and interrupt microaggressions
TPE 6: Developing as a Professional Educator Recognize their own values and implicit and explicit biases, the ways in which these values and implicit and explicit biases may positively and negatively affect teaching and learning, and work to mitigate any negative impact on the teaching and learning of students. They exhibit positive dispositions of caring, support, acceptance, and fairness toward all students and families, as well as toward their colleagues.	Build trusting relationships	∎ Develop rapport ∎ Engage families ∎ Practice reciprocal vulnerability ∎ Employ trauma-informed practices
	Foster self-reflection	∎ Recognize and manage emotional reactions ∎ Examine biases ∎ Explore identity
	Respond constructively across differences	∎ Practice restorative justice ∎ Build capacity to make amends ∎ Identify and interrupt microaggressions

Accreditation Teams

Having new state performance expectations is certainly a powerful step in scaling up a state's efforts to bring social, emotional, and cultural competencies into classrooms. But these standards do not, by themselves, guarantee that university teacher educator programs are addressing them in a meaningful way. The standards will only have weight if the accreditation teams who visit university programs understand them and use them. When the state accreditation team does a site visit, they interview professors, candidates, cooperating teachers, university supervisors, and administrators, and they can ask them what they are doing to address the standards. (The team also reviews written documentation the program has submitted to the state in advance.) Since state accreditation is needed for a program to continue operating, the stakes are high.

But accreditors are not necessarily knowledgeable about or skilled in social, emotional, and cultural competence. The Anchor Competencies Framework provides a common language for accreditation team members, as well as examples of what they should look for when they go on accreditation visits. The framework could serve as a common frame of reference to train and guide individuals tasked with helping to put the new standards in practice, showing them what to look for both in the teacher education classes and in what candidates are doing and talking about in their field assignments. It can also help accreditation teams provide more useful feedback to programs about how to improve their efforts to meet the standards.

As teams begin to assess for social and emotional learning skills implementation in university programs, state commissions on teacher preparation need to consider what is going to count as evidence of effective implementation of social, emotional, and cultural competency standards. At one professional teacher educator conference, we asked the participants, who were in the process of responding to new state standards for an upcoming accreditation visit, what they were doing to ensure that they were meeting the standards. Their responses included such strategies as using a checklist of social and emotional learning practices and requiring one SEL-focused lesson plan to be taught by candidates during their field experience. These efforts are a good start, but we know they are not enough to significantly alter teacher practices, and accreditors need to know that, too, so that they can look deeper.

As the teams look for these standards in the programs they visit, they can, at the same time, gather information to help other programs move forward in this work. The accreditation teams can act as action researchers, encouraging a continuous cycle of inquiry into the integration of socially, emotionally, and culturally competent practices. Asking teacher education faculty for questions they have and challenges they are experiencing in responding to these new standards can lead to the implementation of state-level support for this work. Additionally, they can ask faculty what has helped them meet the standards, so that they share this information with other campuses as well. All of this work will be in the service of building a bridge where all the pieces fit.

Standards for Schools and Students

State education codes have extensive requirements for subjects that will be taught and methods of student discipline in public and private schools. These can be revised to include development of social, emotional, and cultural competencies. CASEL has long advocated for all states to adopt SEL standards, arguing that standards create coherence and uniformity and send clear messages that these competencies are a priority.[4] According to a national scan completed in late 2017, eight US states had articulated SEL standards from kindergarten through grade 12, and sixteen states had guidance and information about SEL on official websites, but had not articulated standards.[5] Interestingly, all fifty states had adopted SEL standards for preschool. The discrepancy is telling. While there is no denying that early childhood is a foundational time for developing social and emotional skills, research we have cited throughout this book makes a compelling case that those skills continue developing throughout childhood and adolescence and are influenced by all the settings in which children and young adults live and learn. Yet policy has paid far less attention to the importance of these skills in the years beyond preschool. The Anchor Competencies Framework, which draws its inspiration from and shares features with the CASEL five competencies that shape standards in Illinois and other states, can be useful for drilling down to not just what students should understand and be able to do, but how teachers can help them get there. It can work in concert with the CASEL work and with existing standards, and also inform the development of standards in states that do not yet have them. Importantly, the Anchor Competencies Framework brings in the vital component of culturally responsive teaching.

State Coalitions

Not all state-level efforts have to be supported or organized by the government. Nonprofit organizations and statewide coalitions are also playing a positive role.[6] For example, CASEL launched its Collaborating States Initiative in 2016, which now includes twenty-five states. Each participating state has been developing plans for implementation of SEL competencies across the spectrum of in-school and out-of-school programs. This work has led California, for example, to develop a set of guidelines for SEL implementation that are being addressed by the California Department of Education.[7]

Another example of a statewide coalition is the Social Emotional Learning Alliance for Massachusetts (SEL4MA). It is a nonprofit created to "advance and support effective social and emotional learning policies and practices" across the state. They advocate for policies and funding, share information about the value of social and emotional learning, and connect stakeholders so they can network and strengthen their own practice as well as their efforts to spread those practices. SEL4MA has a branch called the Massachusetts Consortium for Social-Emotional Learning in Teacher Education (SEL-TEd) that specifically focuses on bringing these efforts into teacher preparation through advocacy and convening. In 2017, SEL-TEd conducted a statewide survey of teacher educators to gather baseline data on current work by teacher educators on SEL skills in teacher preparation programs, and to determine what was needed in order to engage in SEL implementation efforts. Not surprisingly, the advisory committee that conducted the survey reported that faculty felt constrained by state standards, lack of time, and not enough information about how to actually implement SEL within teacher preparation.[8]

This work is not only having an impact in Massachusetts. The survey inspired leaders in California to conduct a similar survey in 2018. The same concerns surfaced in their report.[9] These efforts show the importance of connections and collaboration, not only how multiple states can work together toward a national movement, but also how nonprofit organizations and coalitions can support the work of teacher education, PreK–12 schools, and policy.

DISTRICT LEVEL

School districts are another impetus for change, and they can leverage their authority and support in multiple ways. Consistent with one of the key insights from CASEL's Collaborating District Initiative (CDI), our work has focused on the integration of SEL competencies throughout school districts.[10] The Anchor Competencies Framework provides the blueprint for integration of social, emotional, and cultural competencies throughout the districts. According to CASEL's review of district initiatives to promote social and emotional learning, "there is no single path to successful district implementation. Some [districts we work with] built from the classroom up, using SEL programs. Others built from the central office down, focused on strategy and organization. Some start with clusters of K–12 schools (high school and "feeder" middle and elementary schools). Others rolled out the initiative districtwide at specific grade levels."[11]

The CASEL CDI and the California CORE Districts initiative (see sidebar) have both done significant work in building district capacity, bringing districts together to share what they are learning, and documenting lessons learned about integrating social and emotional competencies into schools. In fact, as noted in an evaluation of the CDI conducted by the American Institutes for Research, "classroom efforts on their own, without broader district support, can show lackluster effects."[12] Superintendents and other district leaders (associate superintendents of curriculum, professional development directors, human resource directors) set priorities and expectations for what happens in their schools and classrooms, as well as the type and amount of support offered to principals and teachers. It is important for them to understand that educators' social, emotional, and cultural competencies are fundamental to student achievement, not a "nice to have" addition to core curriculum. Both the CORE Initiative and CASEL's CDI could use the Anchor Competencies Framework to make a direct connection between SEL and culturally responsive teaching practices. These initiatives could also promote the district's connection with universities to ensure that the preparation of new teachers and new teacher support is consistent with the training offered to veteran teachers in the field.

The following are essential to district change, and can provide guidance to districts beginning this work. We discuss each of these in greater detail below:

- Start with early adopters
- Provide training for district and school site coaches
- Provide professional development for administrators
- Demonstrate to school boards the need to fund and support social, emotional, and cultural competencies
- Make the anchor competencies part of all relevant district job requirements
- Put the anchor competencies into district mission and vision statements
- Incorporate social, emotional, and cultural competencies into district disciplinary policies and procedures

CASEL COLLABORATING DISTRICTS INITIATIVE[13]

Started in 2011, the CASEL Collaborating Districts Initiative (CDI) included eight school districts from across the country (it has since expanded to twenty-one), who, with the help of CASEL consultants and opportunities to learn from each other at Collaborating District meetings, explore various ways to bring SEL skill development into their classrooms throughout the districts. The CASEL competencies of self-awareness, self-management, social awareness, relationship skills, and responsible decision-making guide their work.

The actions underlying CDI's theory of change focus on:

- cultivating commitment to SEL by creating an SEL vision, building central office expertise, aligning resources, and establishing communications
- assessing needs and resources, identifying district SEL needs, and determining resources to support SEL implementation
- supporting SEL programming (providing professional development, establishing SEL standards, integrating SEL with instruction)
- establishing and implementing continuous improvement systems

An American Institutes of Research assessment of outcomes for CDI found the following outcomes.

Improved academics:[14]

- The three districts that use the National Assessment of Educational Progress (Austin, Chicago, and Cleveland) improved their reading and math scores during the CDI implementation years.

- In Anchorage, Austin, Chicago, Cleveland, Oakland, and Nashville, GPAs were higher at the end of the 2015 school year than before the CDI started. The improvements were particularly noticeable in Chicago, going from an average of 2.19 in the three years before the CDI to 2.65 in 2015, an increase of nearly 21 percent.
- Nashville, the only district with consistent standardized tests across the CDI years, showed improvements in both ELA and math achievement.

Improved behavioral outcomes:[15]

- Chicago's graduation rate increased 15 percent during the CDI years.
- Attendance improved in four of six districts that collected this data.
- Suspensions declined in all five of the districts that collected this data.
- Districts also reported that students' social and emotional competence improved, based on student and teacher surveys.

Improved school environment:[16]

- School climate, as measured by district surveys in Chicago and Cleveland, improved during the CDI years. In Anchorage, climate began an upward trajectory before the CDI and sustained that same significant and positive growth during the CDI years.

THE CORE DISTRICTS INITIATIVE[17]

The CORE Districts Initiative was founded in 2010 and includes ten school districts (Clovis, Fresno, Garden Grove, Long Beach, Los Angeles, Oakland, Sacramento City, San Francisco, Sanger, and Santa Ana). This initiative focuses broadly on building and maintaining a comprehensive school improvement and accountability system to provide educators with a clear view of locally provided progress on student-level academic growth, high school readiness, students' social-emotional skills, and schools' culture and climate, along with traditional measures of test scores, graduation rates, and absenteeism. Rather than focusing exclusively on SEL implementation, as CDI has done, the CORE districts place SEL skill development and assessment within a broader effort.

CORE districts have agreed upon four SEL skills that each participating district will address, which are similar to but not the same as the CASEL five competencies (growth mindset, self-management, self-efficacy, and social awareness). Professional development is provided for district and site coaches as well as for administrators to build educators' capacity to bring SEL skills into the classrooms.

The CORE districts, together with PACE (Policy Analysis for California Education, an independent, nonpartisan research center), focus on bringing together local schools and districts to improve student learning. A key focus of the CORE districts is to develop and use an array of more useful measurements to gauge the impact of SEL in schools. CORE, in partnership with PACE, is engaging in research including surveying students in grades 3–12 on their social-emotional learning.

Starting with Early Adopters

One of the most challenging aspects of this work is getting veteran teachers and administrators to see it as central to the future work and identity of the district. For many educators, this is a significant mind shift. They may believe that focusing on student social and emotional needs is not within their purview, that it belongs only in the home or in the office of a therapist.

Our experience suggests that starting with early adopters is a good way to initiate both bottom-up and top-down change. District administrators can begin the work with the most receptive, enthusiastic, and energetic teachers and school leaders. For example, they can form a professional learning community (PLC) that brings together committed educators from across the district. This can help these early adopters deepen and sustain the work and, ultimately, spread the work beyond the PLC. As described in chapter 5, districts who are willing to provide the financial resources and time for this professional development can reap exciting results by seeding the field.

Training for District and School Site Coaches

Many districts have instructional coaches who observe and provide feedback to teachers on a regular basis; these coaches are well positioned to support teachers in incorporating the anchor competencies across the content areas and throughout the year. Some districts have hired and supported coaches specifically dedicated to social and emotional learning. For example, in 2011 the Austin (Texas) Independent School District embarked on an ambitious plan to provide SEL coaching to all school staff. In a systematic rollout, schools were paired with coaches from the district's Department of Social and Emotional Learning for monthly observations and feedback sessions on how effectively they were not only implementing a SEL curricular program but integrating SEL into regular class time.[18]

But districts can also train instructional coaches to incorporate the social, emotional, and cultural lens into the work they are already doing with teachers. This requires screening for these competencies in hiring coaches and also engaging coaches in ongoing professional development to ensure consistency of understanding, language, and approaches to the work. (The observation protocol we described in chapter 3 can be useful for this purpose. Templates are provided in appendixes B and C.)

Professional Development for Administrators

Administrators need to be provided the same professional development opportunities as the teachers (and coaches, when relevant) so that they are all using a common language with one another as well as with students and families. Administrators are often focused on—and challenged by—teachers who are struggling. We suggest that any professional development time needs to help them understand how to use the anchor competencies to work effectively both with teachers who are struggling and with teachers who are ready for new and exciting challenges to remain in the profession.

Administrators come to training sessions with their cell phones on and at the ready for any emergency to which they will have to respond and with a multitude of problems already on their plates. The extent to which the facilitator makes a link between the anchor competencies and how these competencies can help administrators respond to particular challenges will increase the likelihood of principal buy-in. For example, principals will likely have at least one teacher (and perhaps more) who are struggling with classroom discipline issues. By introducing the framework and tools like the observation protocol and then giving them practice looking at and analyzing video clips of teachers whose classrooms are mismanaged and those that are well-managed, they can more effectively structure what they want to say to the teacher as well as what they can offer as specific support.

School Boards

School boards influence the investments that districts make in training and support for teachers and administrators by allocating the necessary budgetary resources. To convince school boards to provide such support, it is important to build the research evidence demonstrating the impact of this work on the quality of the pipeline of teachers coming into districts, the classroom environment, student achievement, and veteran teacher leadership.

School boards are often eager to hear from university faculty and leadership, ideally coordinated with testimony from their own administrators, about the value of efforts that require funding or other kinds of support. For example, university faculty can engage in collaborative research documenting the impact of preservice preparation in the anchor competencies on teachers in their first two years of teaching and share the results at a board meeting. They can offer to come to a school board meeting to share what they are doing in their teacher preparation program to support the development of candidates' social, emotional, and cultural lens. In Sunnyvale, California, Nancy presented at several board meetings over the years to help the district administration get board members excited about the goals they have in place for the integration of the anchor competencies throughout the school district. As a result of these presentations, board members were very supportive of district leadership efforts. One board member even did joint presentations with the district's deputy superintendent of human resources and Nancy at statewide school board conferences to spread the word of the district's work in this area. This demonstrated a real-life connection between the university and the district and facilitated the university's ability to select placements for teacher candidates consistent with the goals of the university program.

Job Qualifications

Clearly articulating the need for commitment to and skill in social, emotional, and cultural competence in the classroom and the work of administrators sends a powerful, essential message to potential candidates for these positions. Those not oriented toward these competencies or whose beliefs and assumptions about teaching and learning are inconsistent with attention to these competencies then get the message that they need not apply.

In Atlanta Public Schools, for example, superintendent Meria Carstarphen makes it clear that all staff, from maintenance staff and bus drivers to teachers and administrators, should be knowledgeable about social and emotional learning and how to nurture it. In an interview in 2018, she said, "We have changed the way we hire and onboard people. When I interview principals and hire people who report directly to me, we talk about school culture and behavior expectations. It's bigger than ethics and human resources policies. It's about the culture we want to create and making sure they share our district's vision."[19] She went on to talk about expanding this expectation beyond the administrative team: "As the superintendent, I participate in all new employees' training. If you are new to our district, you are going to meet me, and we are going to discuss SEL and school culture and what is expected. I role-play the part of a student, and I go up to one of the new hires—it could be a mechanic or a teacher—and I make some smart-aleck comment and then ask, 'How would you show me you care about me? What would you say to me?'"[20]

District Mission and Vision Statements

A district that articulates explicit goals related to social, emotional, and cultural competencies will have a roadmap to guide the kinds of decisions they make and how they communicate across the district stakeholders. For example, Sunnyvale School District puts it this way: "Our mission is to provide every student with a strong foundation of academic, behavioral, and social-emotional skills to prepare them for success in a diverse, challenging, and changing world."[21] But a mission statement is just the beginning. It must be backed by real commitment and action. Many schools and districts say that they strive to educate "the whole child" but do not have an intentional or coherent approach to doing so.

District Procedures Addressing Student Behavioral Issues

Districts typically set guidelines for how teachers and administrators will respond to student behavioral issues. Student study teams (SST, sometimes called student assistance teams or student support teams) are commonly used in districts across the US as one of the early steps to support a child who is struggling academically or behaviorally in school. Sacramento School District is typical in describing the SST as a positive, team-oriented approach to assist students with a wide range of concerns related to their school performance and experience. The purpose of the SST is to identify and intervene early in order to design a support system for students having difficulty in the general education classroom. Either a staff member or parent can make a referral. The team usually includes a parent or caretaker, teacher, administrator, and support personnel, and sometimes a counselor or special education teacher. The SST meeting provides everyone with an opportunity to share concerns and develop a plan. If the SST team determines that the child could have a special need, they may recommend a formal special education assessment. Follow-up meetings are scheduled to ensure that the plan is working and to make adjustments to ensure that students can succeed and reach their potential.[22]

One of the challenges of this support system is providing a range of options that can be implemented by the teacher and successfully support the student. Student study teams usually focus on the academic struggles or behavior issues that the student is exhibiting. Imagine how rich the data gathering, discussion, and choice of strategies might be if the Anchor Competencies Framework was used. The teacher would first use the anchor competencies to guide the observation notes of the student, both in class and in other spaces like the cafeteria and hallways. The student's parents or caretaker could be asked to use the anchors to guide their observations of the child at home. The group could then, in addition to discussing academic challenges and/or behavioral issues, talk about what they observe related to each of the seven anchor competencies. After agreeing on which anchors are particularly in need of attention, the team would have a guide of possible teacher moves and corresponding specific teaching strategies based on the framework.

UNIVERSITY LEVEL

Through their training of both teachers and educational leaders, universities can encourage the educational ecosystem to institutionalize social, emotional and cultural competencies in classrooms. We discuss each of the suggested strategies to support change efforts in greater detail below:

- Sponsor Teacher Educator Institutes
- Provide opportunities for professional development to university field supervisors
- Raise standards for cooperating teacher selection and provide professional development to cooperating teachers
- Embed the Anchor Competencies Framework in university advanced degree programs

- Include social, emotional, and cultural competencies in appropriate job requirements
- Promote hiring of diverse faculty and selection of a diverse teacher candidate pool

Teacher Educator Professional Development

CRTWC developed a yearlong Teacher Educator Institute (TEI) as a method for disseminating the Anchor Competencies Framework and supporting faculty from various institutions in bringing the framework to their departments. Universities are encouraged to have a team of faculty members participate in the TEI and to provide a letter of support from their dean or chair. The program includes on-site retreats, three days in length, at the beginning and end of the academic year, along with four video-conference meetings during the course of the year to provide further opportunities to discuss ideas across institutions, and to continue professional development related to the use of the anchors. At each in-person and virtual meeting, CRTWC staff engage faculty in activities and discussions that they can then use with their colleagues and teacher candidates. All videos and case studies are made available for faculty to use for these purposes.

Faculty who have participated in the Institutes have taken diverse approaches to incorporating the framework. With strong support and direction from their dean to bring social, emotional, and cultural competencies into their programs, six faculty members from the University of Dayton participated in the TEI. Upon their return to their home campus, they asked for time at a faculty meeting to share what they were learning, particularly focusing on an introduction to the Anchor Competencies Framework. The dean encouraged them to spend time at every monthly faculty meeting over the course of the year discussing their work with the TEI and helping their colleagues incorporate the framework.

Later in the year, the broader cohort team collaborated to complete the Anchor Competencies Program Matrix (see chapter 4) to be strategic about threading the strategies throughout the program. Several faculty members also presented at conferences and wrote articles about their work with the TEI.[23]

Several faculty teams began the work at their home institutions by conducting a baseline survey to determine: (1) the extent to which social, emotional, and cultural competencies were currently evident across the program; (2) what faculty already knew about social, emotional, and cultural competencies; and (3) what supports they would like in order to further integrate these competencies into their teaching. A common issue that emerged is a wide variation in understanding, terminology, and beliefs about these competencies among faculty at the same institution. This survey data established the need for a more consistent approach, based on detailed discussions about the Anchor Competencies Framework.

Through external evaluations, we have found that key ingredients to the success of the Teacher Educator Institutes include leadership support at the home campus, adequate time both during and outside of the TEI retreats for discussion and planning, and ongoing support and mentoring from CRTWC staff. Many of our participants have noted that they need to spend more time than they thought on just understanding the social, emotional, and cultural lens themselves in order to share it with colleagues and use it effectively with candidates. One of the biggest benefits of the TEI is the gift of dedicated time and space for reflecting on this important but challenging work.

Several faculty members from a program in the Midwest (one that has state SEL standards for teachers) shared that before they participated in the TEI, having no specific examples of how to bring SEL into the program, they fell back on providing a checklist of what candidates had to do, including writing and teaching a SEL skill lesson as one of the program requirements. Participation in the TEI provided positive support, the opportunity to learn from those at other institutions, and a roadmap for addressing the SEL standards across the program.

Professional Development for University Field Supervisors

University field supervisors are generally only loosely tethered to the teacher preparation program. They are often not paid to do anything other than to observe candidates in the field and lead field experience seminar courses. This causes a serious problem with building that sturdy bridge we referred to at the beginning of this chapter. If these field supervisors are not knowledgeable about the faculty's goals and overarching strategies, they are likely not going to provide consistent content in either their teaching or observation of candidates in the field.

The way in which Dr. Dena Sexton, director of candidate field placements at San José State University, handled the challenge of little paid time to bring supervisors together was to offer them an opportunity to participate in a year-long learning community on social, emotional, and cultural competencies for their own interest. Because this opportunity was voluntary, she was essentially bringing together early adopters. Ten of the seventeen supervisors chose to attend, perhaps because they were eager to take advantage of the rare professional learning opportunity. Dr. Sexton provided a set of readings, and the meetings were held in online video conferences to make it more feasible for the supervisors, who often traveled to multiple school sites and sometimes had other jobs as well, to participate. The results were exciting. All ten supervisors stayed with the program for the entire year and asked to continue it the next year.

Standards for Cooperating Teacher Selection and Their Professional Development

As we described in chapter 4, laying the groundwork in preservice teacher education requires a commitment to respond to the challenge of ensuring that the cooperating teachers with whom universities work exhibit the skills consistent with program goals. Again, the need for a common language and framework at the university and in the districts with which the university collaborates will make a significant difference in the sturdiness and usability of the bridge.

One teacher preparation program option at SJSU increased the status of being a cooperating teacher by using a different title, "faculty associate," instituting an application process for the position and providing an enhanced stipend (thanks to a local foundation grant). The application process included responding to a written set of questions, participating in an interview with someone from the university and the district, and having their site administrator separately submit an evaluation of their teaching using a state-developed rubric. Universities often feel they must rely on the districts alone to decide who will be a cooperating teacher. We suggest that if the university makes a point of developing a trusting relationship and creates community with the districts in its service area, there is a much higher chance that districts will be willing and even excited to work together to select and train cooperating teachers. University-district advisory board meetings where issues are discussed and decided collaboratively, and where competencies for being a cooperating teacher and the process of selection are developed collaboratively, have made a huge difference in our experience.

University Advanced Degree Programs

District leaders are more likely to develop the needed awareness, understanding, and commitment if they are exposed to the framework during masters and doctoral programs. University programs could provide opportunities for specialization in social, emotional, and cultural competencies just as they do in other areas. Further, we suggest that rather than separating out social justice, culturally responsive, or culturally sustaining pedagogy from social-emotional learning, schools of education should design program specializations that bring them together, possibly using the anchor framework as a guide. If educational leaders come to school sites with foundational knowledge and a commitment to the use of a social, emotional, and cultural lens in their schools, if they can look to hire new teachers who have been prepared in programs that integrate the use of this lens in teacher preparation, imagine what could happen!

Social, Emotional, and Cultural Competence in Faculty Job Descriptions

As we suggest for districts, university teacher education positions will increase a common focus by including attention to social, emotional, and cultural competencies as part of job qualifications. For example, as part of a tenure-track job description at San José State University's Teacher Education Department, attention to the social and emotional dimensions of teaching and learning was listed as one of the desired job qualifications: "Knowledge of and commitment to integrating social-emotional dimensions of teaching and learning in teaching practices." The department found that even though it was categorized as "desirable" rather than required, it led to extremely helpful discussions with candidates.[24]

PROMOTE HIRING OF DIVERSE FACULTY AND SELECTION OF A DIVERSE TEACHER CANDIDATE POOL

There is a critical need to ensure a rich diversity of educators that is comparable to the diversity of children in our classrooms. The numbers indicate that our classrooms are increasingly filled with students representing hundreds of different cultures and languages. Yet, as research done in US public schools in 2014 documents, although the percentage of Latinx, Black, Asian, and other students of color far exceeded that of White students, 84 percent of their teachers were White.[25] To ensure that more teachers of color are in classrooms, we need to proactively bring them into and support them in teacher preparation programs. Just as in our K–12 schools, teacher candidates of color need to see professors, university supervisors, and cooperating teachers who reflect their own racial, cultural, and linguistic backgrounds. To do so, the teacher preparation programs need to aggressively examine their faculty hiring and support policies and procedures to ensure a diversity of thinking, perspectives, and experiences that can lead to rich and challenging conversations and programmatic efforts that, in turn, attract more teachers of color into the profession.[26]

POLICY FRAMEWORK AND UNDERLYING BELIEFS AND ASSUMPTIONS

Those who are reforming policies and structures need to be mindful of how difficult it is to micromanage how their efforts will ultimately affect students. There are countless situations in schools that cannot be foreseen, but that will be addressed more coherently and consistently when the entire educational system employs the social, emotional, and cultural lens. Therefore, it is important at all levels to constantly explore beliefs and assumptions, consistent with the anchor framework. The following is a cautionary tale of how the best of intentions can be derailed when a common vision of a school grounded in social, emotional, and cultural competencies is not shared by everyone.

A struggling suburban high school with a diverse student population spent years working on the development of small learning communities of students with faculty working in instructional teams within these communities, winning awards for its efforts. Supportive relationships between students and teachers, among students, and among teachers were strongly encouraged. So, two of the anchors, building trusting relationships and creating community, were emphasized. The school also promoted the use of projects that required student collaboration, another anchor competency. How teachers respond when a student experiences difficulties can sometimes provide data as to whether teachers have deeply committed to the assumptions and beliefs that support these anchors.

An academically very capable, straight A student, Shawn, became ill during fall semester of his junior year and missed the entire month of classes in November and part of December. This led Shawn not to want to return to school for fear of being too far behind. The parents made several attempts to contact each teacher without success. The principal took the responsibility of communicating with all the teachers and relayed to the parents and student that his assignments would be modified so that he would not fall behind. But Shawn withdrew from classes during the spring semester. Why did this happen? Why didn't Shawn return to school second semester? While the school was structured into learning communities to support the students, teachers generally believed that larger-scale support for a student needed to go through the principal. However, this was not communicated by anyone to the student, so the student interpreted their method of communication as not caring.

What if this situation had played out differently? What if the team of teachers in the learning community and the school counselor had met with the principal to discuss how Shawn had been doing prior to his illness and which adult at the school had the strongest relationship with him, who could therefore serve as the key support person? That support person would then invite Shawn to a one-on-one meeting to discuss what Shawn felt he needed in terms of support from his teachers and the sincere desire of the teachers to support him. What if, at this meeting, the support person used strategies to encourage development of Shawn's competencies of perseverance and growth mindset? Addressing the situation in this way would likely have also strengthened a trusting relationship with the student. Imagine Shawn's response to his situation if he was being told that his teachers understood that this had been a difficult time, and that it was hard for him to return, but that they had his back and would be there to support him. And, further, that they would provide the supports he said he needed.

If these teachers had adopted a social, emotional, and cultural lens they likely would have responded to this unique situation in a more productive way that also would have led to additional student learning. It is impossible to lay out in detail the steps teachers and administrators should take for every possible challenge. Schools—and life—are too complicated. But if the policies and organizational structures (the well-designed bridge between theory and practice) are organized for a more supportive educational system, it is more likely that teachers and administrators will be empowered to handle the multitude of challenges they face more effectively and gracefully.

The research summarized in this book shows we know what to do. It's a matter of designing and constructing the bridge, and then crossing over it, to get from that point to more effective practice. There is a role for all parties in this vital effort.

CHAPTER 7

A Vision for the Future

USING THE SOCIAL, emotional, and cultural anchor competencies serves as a roadmap to help educators develop and use a lens that guides the planning, data gathering, and decision-making needed to provide a safe and equitable classroom environment where both students and teachers can retain resilience and a sense of optimism, where all students experience academic success, and where children learn to take responsibility for the common good. Use of the Anchor Competencies Framework across the professional development pipeline will support informed and effective teacher practice, but it will require patient, consistent, and comprehensive work at all levels of the education system. We recognize that our approach of bringing together social, emotional, and cultural competencies is a significant departure from what is commonly seen in schools today—a short-term approach with a tendency to focus on discrete student SEL lessons, provide SEL programs to address these competencies within school districts, and add one or more SEL competencies to teacher performance expectations. However, we argue that the focus on the teacher professional development pipeline is essential if, as a society, we are to make systemic change that outlasts turnover in school and district leadership. The investment in a pipeline approach to teaching through a social, emotional, and cultural lens represents a new way of educating students—one that places a core emphasis on relationships, resilience, and valuing all adults and children in the community as unique individuals with the potential to succeed. This is particularly important given the rampant turnover in American schools for all personnel, from teachers to principals to superintendents, and the fragmented, ever-changing nature of education reform.[1] We simply cannot rely on a charismatic leader or a well-designed program to institutionalize changes in the way our students need. Steadily and consistently building the competence of teachers and administrators throughout the system may not be flashy, but if it sticks and it spreads, it has real potential to spark an educational revolution.

REVISITING A CASE STUDY: THINKING LONG-TERM

In chapter 1, we shared the story of two novice teachers—who attended the same teacher education program but then began their careers in two very different elementary schools—to illustrate the importance of all educational institutions reinforcing the social, emotional, and cultural lens. Susan was supported in her first year by colleagues and supervisors who believed in the importance of social, emotional, and cultural competence and ended the year energized by the success of her students and school. In contrast, Maria was so stressed by her students' behavior challenges, her colleagues' harsh disciplinary techniques, and her school's negative climate that she was considering leaving the profession. When Suzanne talked to Maria at the end of that year, she was worried for her and for her students. When she followed up a few years later, Maria's story had some lows but ultimately some highs.

Maria's second year of teaching continued to be a struggle, particularly when she taught summer school, which she describes as "really horrible," because her students acted out so much. She says, "I did it for twenty-five or twenty-seven days, and I dreaded every day," but she hung on with the support of another teacher who would stop in frequently to share strategies for working with her rowdy students.

When she began her third year, she said, she was "drained and tired, and I said, 'No one is going to mess with me.' I was so strict. I didn't take any BS from anyone." She spoke sharply to students and handed out consequences as soon as a student acted in a way that didn't conform to expectations. But Maria realized she had finally been assigned a group of students who had more self-regulation skills, and who didn't have such severe behavioral challenges. "By

October, I realized I didn't need to be so strict. I started building relationships with those kids," and she began to relax and rely on the social and emotional skills to which she had always felt committed. She found herself frequently going back to things she had learned in a preservice course about building relationships with students. She focused on community-building strategies and began connecting with students one-on-one, for example about what they did on the weekends. She made a point to say "Good morning" to each child every morning and to tell them "I missed you" when they were absent. She began to see a difference in her students—and in herself. They all began to show more respect for one another—and to learn.

Maria brought her relationship building and other social and emotional strategies into her fourth year of teaching, which turned out to be with another highly challenging group of fifth graders. She describes that class as immature, "emotionally needy," prone to frequent meltdowns about their struggles with classwork, and very disrespectful, especially in their use of explicit language. But, she says, "I'm able to handle it a lot better. The respect is there [between me and the students]. And there's a lot more teaching going on."

Relationship building continues to be her foundation. "At the beginning, you have to set the tone, the rules, the procedures, but then the relationships you need to continue building all year," she explains. She also works on building growth mindset and self-efficacy by showing them videos, reinforcing it in her feedback, and asking them, "Would you talk to a friend the way you are talking to yourself right now?" She found that the students really liked hearing her read out loud, and she began selecting books about kindness or with an "SEL message," like one about a girl with dyslexia who felt ostracized by her peers. She says she strikes a balance between these supportive strategies and laying down the rules. "I don't let disrespect slide," she says, and she always calls them out for bad language. But "I apologize for my own mistakes" to model that, and "I'm more lenient on things like following all the rules" if a child who is struggling does the best she can and isn't hurting anyone.

All of these strategies, she believes, have made a big difference with her students. By the end of the year, she said, "I have the best fifth-grade class. I take pride in that and I tell them that all the time. A student today said, 'It feels so good to come in here. It feels like home and I feel so safe.' I said, 'Well, you *should* feel safe when you come here!' They aren't going to learn if they don't feel comfortable with me."

Maria points to her success with one student in particular, a boy named David. "David came in from the other [fifth-grade] class and is the toughest kid. He caused riots in the other classroom, for example, by sitting in the teacher's chair and telling her he wasn't going to move. The teachers tried everything with him—a behavior plan with stickers, rewards—he did nothing. He was suspended two or three times, and one time I saw him in the office, and I realized he was just going to sit there and bother the secretaries all day. So I asked the principal if it was okay to invite David to my class. When he came in to my class, I treated David the same as all my other students [with a positive attitude and expectations]. When he was off task, I would tap his shoulder or something so I'm not calling him out in front of everyone; David doesn't need that, he's had enough of that from other teachers."

David immediately warmed to Maria and the way she approached him with positive intent. "He did everything with zero break cards, zero disruption. He was an angel. After a few days, he kept asking to come back, and I asked him if he wanted to stay for the rest of the year. He's been in my class ever since, and I've built this really good relationship with him. Yesterday they made cards for someone special in their life and he made it for me. Now he takes off his hood within a minute of getting in class, and he's wearing colors [instead of all black] for the first time. A kid told me, 'You changed David. He hit me, but then he apologized.'" Moreover, she continued, David had just scored his highest ever in math and reading.

With the foundation in the anchor competencies that she received during her teacher education program, Maria was able to navigate many challenges and help her students, even the toughest among them, thrive. That foundation was strong enough for the skills she needed to reemerge after a few years—a powerful impact that is surely gratifying to the faculty who taught her in the preservice program. But if Maria had had the kind of support in the anchor competencies received by her former classmate, Susan, those first few years might not have put her at such high risk for burnout or resulted in lost time for her students.

And what about next year, when David moves to sixth grade? Neither we nor Maria can predict the future for him, or for any student. But we all hope that he connects with another teacher who has the same social, emotional, and culturally competent lens and strategies as Maria. If he does, we believe his positive trajectory is likely to continue upward. If he doesn't, there is a real risk of him sliding back into his old habits. And as he gets older, the consequences for inappropriate behavior and low achievement are likely to get heftier, possibly even putting him at risk for an all-too-common cycle of disengagement and limited opportunities for a stable and successful adulthood.

Our vision is for all educators to have consistent, ongoing support to integrate the social, emotional, and cultural anchors in their everyday teaching so that all students can thrive from year to year, whether their teachers are brand new to the classroom or veteran educators who have to continue to find the energy and inspiration to keep teaching year after year.

CONDITIONS FOR SUCCESS

For this vision to become reality, everyone in the educational system—teachers, administrators, professional development staff, university faculty, and others—must keep the following tenets of the framework front and center: (1) understanding the individual, family, community, cultural, and sociopolitical contexts in which this work must occur; (2) bringing social and emotional learning and culturally responsive pedagogy together; and (3) leveraging the full career and professional development continuum to ensure that this lens can and will be used by those entrusted with our children and by the children themselves.

A number of conditions will help educators at all levels stay focused and put these pieces in place:

- a common language and collaboration
- champions for change
- sufficient time
- research that will help identify and refine the most effective approaches

Common Language and Collaboration

Shared terminology can support clear communication among education stakeholders and create consistency in an area that is often seen as fuzzy or hard to define. In preservice, for instance, we have seen the value of having faculty members, candidates, and cooperating teachers understand and use the same language and model and use compatible strategies.

Of course, creating this kind of consistency is a longstanding challenge in education, not the least when it comes to social, emotional, and cultural competencies that have been variously referred to as SEL, character education, noncognitive skills, bullying prevention, positive youth development, academic mindset, and many other terms. The Anchor Competencies Framework spells out specific skills and the steps needed to develop them in order to create and support consistency across these many initiatives, rather than competing with them.

For example, one way that some preservice teacher preparation programs begin is to provide a full-day orientation to all incoming teacher candidates and their cooperating teachers. During the day, candidates and their cooperating teachers participate in activities such as learning what each other's favored communication style is so they can decide how questions and feedback can be shared in a way that meets both their needs. Even this typical exercise can be framed explicitly in the terms of the Anchor Competencies Framework so that cooperating teachers and the teacher preparation program can model efforts to build trust and clear communications. As another example, in university-district partnerships we have seen success with creating time for all parties to meet and view a video of a lesson, and then analyze it together using the social, emotional, and cultural competencies as a guide and a common language.

Clearly, collaboration goes hand-in-hand with communicating in a common language, but it requires more than that. It requires breaking some of the unwritten codes that discourage collaboration, including the individualistic culture of university departments that keeps faculty from knowing what is occurring in other courses, and the outdated and ineffective method of professional development that confines teachers to one-day workshops.

Champions for Change

In our experience, systemic, sustained change requires high-level leadership and support from district leaders and university deans and department chairs. It is ideal to begin this work with the support of multiple champions, such as both the dean and department chair at local teaching institutions that provide the bulk of new teachers. However, we have also seen the work take off with the support of just one leader or a core group of teachers or faculty (two to six people) who carry out the change process and generate interest and support from others. There is definitely room for optimism. Of the thirteen institutions who participated in the CRTWC Teacher Educator Institute from 2017 to 2019, nine have begun making significant inroads in integrating the anchor competencies in their own courses, their teacher education programs, or both. As we described in chapter 6, cooperating teachers can also become early adopters who then become the district teacher leaders, spreading the work throughout the district.

Time

There is no substitute for providing adequate time to develop the social, emotional, and cultural lens. In our work with both university faculty and school staff, we have heard over and over again about the need for modeling, opportunities for practice, and group discussions to identify and implement next steps—all of which take time and intentionality. Furthermore, the fundamental work of building trusting relationships, exploring assumptions, and reflecting, which are so fundamental to the Anchor Competencies Framework, cannot be rushed or crammed into a one-day workshop. These ideas have to marinate and then evolve over time. Ongoing, sustained professional learning is therefore paramount.

Research

Research on both implementation and impact is important for justifying investments in this work and for continued development of knowledge and best practices. For example, we acknowledge that we need research studying the impact of using the framework in teacher preparation on the practice of new graduates and their students. Do they stay in the profession longer if they have been prepared to use the social, emotional, and cultural lens in their practice? What are effective and efficient ways that integration of these competencies can be scaled to teacher preparation programs across the country? To what extent can this work be done online through video meetings, and to what extent do participants need face to face contact? What correlations can be made between integration of these competencies into teacher practice and student academic achievement and a positive school climate?

TEACHING "FULL HUMANS"

The benefits of making these commitments and applying the Anchor Competencies Framework are well worth the effort required. This approach is one that targets student success broadly, equipping students with the skills to: succeed in core academics, develop the agency and self-efficacy they need to be engaged in learning and find a path for the future, form positive relationships that are the basis for current and future social adjustment, bolster their own mental health to prevent intra- and interpersonal problems, and beyond. In other words, the social, emotional, and cultural anchor competencies are fundamental to teaching and learning.

The changes the framework can spur have been summed up best, we think, by Nancy Myers, senior lecturer in education and director of the California Reading and Literature Project at California Lutheran University. Myers began using the framework with teacher candidates during her participation as a Fellow in the 2017–18 Teacher Educator Institute. When she connected with each of the candidates one-on-one at the end of her course, she asked them to share what they found most important or surprising over the semester. One told her, "Before this class, I thought I was becoming a teacher to fill their [the students'] heads with knowledge. But now I see they are not just brains, but full humans." The professor responded, "Yes, and so are you!" She went on to tell us: "Thank goodness we are doing this. If they didn't have this experience, and they went into teaching like that, the children would have been forgotten in all the focus on standards. Getting this from the very beginning is so essential for them to be caring teachers and caring human beings."

Whatever role we play in education, we must see those we teach and mentor— and those who teach and mentor us—as full humans. Anything less is not enough.

Lesson Plan Template

Name	_____	Lesson Date	_____
Grade Level	_____	School	_____
Subject	_____	Cooperating Teacher	_____

Lesson Rationale:

(Why do these students need this lesson at this time?)

Common Core Standard(s):

www.cde.ca.gov/re/cc/:

English Language Development Standard(s):

English Language Development Objective(s):

Content/Subject Objective(s):

(*What do you want students to specifically learn as a result of this lesson?*)

Social, emotional, and cultural competencies:

(*What anchor competencies do students need to be successful in this lesson? How will they be taught, modeled, or reviewed?*)

Time (Pacing)	Step-by-Step Procedure (Instructional Sequence)	Where lesson plan elements are addressed (CCSS, ELD, Differentiation, Anchors, Formative & Summative Assessments)
	Introduction/Hook	
	Content Instruction	
	Closure/Wrap-Up/Reflection	

Observation Protocol Template #1
Social, Emotional, and Cultural Competencies

IMPLEMENTATION GUIDELINES

1. Teacher candidate decides focus for observation and establishes "context" for observer.
2. Fill in evidence for the anchor competencies that apply. It is not expected that there will be evidence for all anchor competencies during any one lesson.
3. Consider the amount of classroom experience of the teacher candidate when observing, since first semester teacher candidates may only be in the classroom a few days per week and may not have had much teaching time.
4. The Observation Protocol is intended to serve as a tool for discussion, formative feedback, and development of a teacher's social, emotional, and cultural lens.
5. Observers should note that shifts away from the planned lesson may be desirable, demonstrating flexibility and the ability to respond in alternative, more productive ways than planned.
6. Consider that use of the anchor competencies is, in part, an academic intervention, and observe for their integration into content/curriculum where possible or needed.
7. Teachers are not expected to prepare an "SEL lesson," but to demonstrate places in their practice where anchor competencies are integrated to facilitate student success and ability to thrive.

CRTWC Classroom Observation Protocol			
Date: ____/_____/____	Start time: _____AM/PM	End time: _____AM/PM	School:
Teacher:	Subject observed:	Grade level(s):	Total # of students:
# Female:	# Male:	# EL students:	# Students with learning disabilities:

Lesson Plan Design	Notes
1. Includes attention to the anchor competencies and accompanying teacher move(s) that students need to be successful in this lesson.	
2. Describes how the necessary social, emotional, and cultural competencies will be explicitly taught/ modeled, if needed.	
3. The lesson plan includes opportunities for student reflection.	

Teacher candidate completes prior to lesson:

1. Focus issue for observation:

2. Teacher's Individual Context:

Directions: Take notes in the right column regarding evidence of anchor competencies. Remember it is not expected that there will be evidence of all the anchor competencies or teacher moves in any one lesson.

Anchor Competencies and Teacher Moves	Notes/Evidence/Scripting

1. Build trusting relationships
  a. Develop rapport
  b. Engage families
  c. Practice reciprocal vulnerability
  d. Employ trauma informed practices	

2. Foster self-reflection
  a. Recognize and manage emotional reactions
  b. Examine biases
  c. Explore identity	

3. Foster growth mindset
  a. Articulates affirming counter-narratives
  b. Shift to positive self-talk
  c. Connect learning to the brain	

4. Cultivate perseverance
  a. Provide asset-based formative feedback
  b. Set and monitor goals
  c. Embrace productive struggles	

5. Create classroom community
  a. Attend to status issues
  b. Foster individual voice
  c. Create a culture of engagement
  d. Affirm each other's assets	

6. Promote collaborative learning
  a. Practice building consensus
  b. Engage in structured academic and social conversations
  c. Practice reflective listening	

7. Respond constructively across differences
  a. Practice restorative justice
  b. Builds capacity to make amends
  c. Identify and interrupt micro-aggressions	

Summary/Reflections:

Use this space to have a post-observation conversation with the teacher candidate to discuss strengths, areas for growth, and next steps.

Strengths	Area(s) for growth	Next steps

Used with permission by Center for Reaching & Teaching the Whole Child.

Observation Protocol Template #2
Social, Emotional, and Cultural Competencies

IMPLEMENTATION GUIDELINES

1. Teacher candidate decides focus for observation and establishes "context" for observer.
2. Fill in evidence for the anchor competencies that apply. It is not expected that there will be evidence for all anchor competencies during any one lesson.
3. Consider the amount of classroom experience of the teacher candidate when observing, since first semester teacher candidates may only be in the classroom a few days per week and may not have had much teaching time.
4. The Observation Protocol is intended to serve as a tool for discussion, formative feedback, and development of a teacher's social, emotional, and cultural lens.
5. Observers should note that shifts away from the planned lesson may be desirable, demonstrating flexibility and the ability to respond in alternative, more productive ways than planned.
6. Consider that use of the anchor competencies is, in part, an academic intervention, and observe for their integration into content/curriculum where possible or needed.
7. Teachers are not expected to prepare an "SEL lesson," but to demonstrate places in their practice where anchor competencies are integrated to facilitate student success and ability to thrive.

CRTWC Classroom Observation Protocol			
Date: ____/____/____	Start time: _____AM/PM	End time: _____AM/PM	School:
Teacher:	Subject observed:	Grade level(s):	Total # of students:
# Female:	# Male:	# EL Students:	# Students with learning disabilities:

Lesson Plan Design	Notes
1. Includes attention to the anchor competencies and accompanying teacher move(s) that students need to be successful in this lesson.	
2. Describes how the necessary social, emotional, and cultural competencies will be explicitly taught/ modeled, if needed.	
3. The lesson plan includes opportunities for student reflection.	

Teacher candidate completes prior to lesson:

1. Focus issue for observation:

2. Teacher's Individual Context:

Directions: After scripting teacher behavior on the left, draw arrows to anchor competencies and teacher moves on the right. Color code to indicate the PRIMARY teacher move you think the teacher explicitly intended to demonstrate, according to their requested "focus issue."

Script Evidence of Anchor Competencies	Anchor Competencies & Teacher Moves

	1. **Build trusting relationships**
	  a. Develop rapport
	  b. Engage families
	  c. Practice reciprocal vulnerability
	  d. Employ trauma informed practices
	2. **Foster self-reflection**
	  a. Recognize and manage emotional reactions
	  b. Examine biases
	  c. Explore identity
	3. **Foster growth mindset**
	  a. Articulates affirming counter-narratives
	  b. Shift to positive self-talk
	  c. Connect learning to the brain
	4. **Cultivate perseverance**
	  a. Provide asset-based formative feedback
	  b. Set and monitor goals
	  c. Embrace productive struggles
	5. **Create community**
	  a. Attend to status issues
	  b. Foster individual voice
	  c. Create a culture of engagement
	  d. Affirm each other's assets
	6. **Promote collaborative learning**
	  a. Practice building consensus
	  b. Engage in structured academic and social conversations
	  c. Practice reflective listening
	7. **Respond constructively across differences**
	  a. Practice restorative justice
	  b. Builds capacity to make amends
	  c. Identify and interrupt micro-aggressions

Additional Observer Notes:	

Summary/Reflections:

Use this space to have a post-observation conversation with the teacher candidate to discuss strengths, areas for growth, and next steps.

Strengths	Area(s) for growth	Next steps

Course Matrix Template
Social, Emotional, and Cultural Competencies

Name of Course: _____

Directions: Use the matrix to identify which anchor competencies and which parts of the lens development process you use in your class to support teacher candidates in developing the competencies themselves and in integrating them into their teaching practice. Put an "X" in the boxes that apply. Typically, you will not be putting an "X" in all the boxes for any given class. For example, if you model, provide practice, give assignments to candidates to try teaching cooperative learning skills in their field assignment, and then have them come back to your seminar to reflect on what they learned, you would put an "X" in the appropriate boxes under *Promote Cooperative Learning*.

Course matrix

Developing social, emotional, and cultural anchor competencies	Build Trusting Relationships	Foster Self-Reflection	Foster Growth Mindset	Cultivate Perseverance	Create Community	Promote Collaborative Learning	Respond Constructively Across Differences
Explore assumptions and beliefs							
Model							
Provide practice							
Provide opportunity for reflection							

Program Matrix Template

Social, Emotional, and Cultural Competencies

Fill in the boxes below identifying where in your program (specific courses, fieldwork assignments) each of the 7 Anchor Competencies are explicitly taught by exploring both teacher and students' assumptions, providing modeling, opportunities for practice, and reflection.

Program matrix

Developing social, emotional, and cultural anchor competencies	Build Trusting Relationships	Foster Self-Reflection	Foster Growth Mindset	Cultivate Perseverance	Create Collaborative Community	Promote Collaborative Learning	Respond Constructively Across Differences
Explore Assumptions and beliefs							
Model							
Provide practice							
Provide opportunity for reflection							

Notes

PREFACE

1. John Bridgeland, Mary Bruce, and Arya Hariharan, *The Missing Piece: A National Teacher Survey on How Social and Emotional Learning Can Empower Children and Transform Schools. A Report for CASEL* (Chicago: CASEL, 2016), https://casel.org/wp-content/uploads/2016/01/the-missing-piece.pdf.

2. Sarah Schwartz, "Teachers Support Social-Emotional Learning But Say Students in Distress Strain their Skills," *Education Week* 38 (2019): 37, https://www.edweek.org/ew/articles/2019/07/17/teachers-support-social-emotional-learning-but-say-students.html.

3. Stephanie M. Jones and Jennifer Kahn, *The Evidence Base for How We Learn: Supporting Students' Social, Emotional, and Academic Development: Consensus Statements of Evidence from the Council of Distinguished Scientists* (Washington, DC: National Commission on Social, Emotional, and Academic Development and the Aspen Institute, 2017).

4. Stephanie M. Jones and Suzanne M. Bouffard, "Social and Emotional Learning in Schools: From Programs to Strategies," *Social Policy Report* 26, no. 4 (2012): 1–22; Joseph A. Durlak et al., eds., *Handbook of Social and Emotional Learning* (New York: Guilford Press, 2015); C. Cybele Raver, Pamela W. Garner, and Radiah Smith-Donald, "The Roles of Emotional Regulation and Emotion Knowledge for Children's Academic Readiness: Are the Links Causal?" in *School Readiness and the Transition to Kindergarten in the Era of Accountability*, ed. R. C. Pianta, M. J. Cox, and K. L. Snow (Baltimore, MD: Paul H. Brookes Publishing, 2007), 121–147, https://psycnet.apa.org/record/2007-03648-007.

5. Abigail Hess, "These Are the Most In-Demand Skills of 2019, According to LinkedIn," CNBC (website), January 8, 2019, https://www.cnbc.com/2019/01/07/the-most-in-demand-skill-of-2019-according-to-linkedin.html.

6. Jennifer L. DePaoli et al., *Respected: Perspectives of Youth on High School & Social and Emotional Learning* (Chicago: CASEL, 2018), https://casel.org/wp-content/uploads/2018/11/Respected.pdf.

7. Christina D. Bethell et al., *Issue Brief: A National and Across State Profile on Adverse Childhood Experiences Among Children and Possibilities to Heal and Thrive* (Baltimore, MD: Johns Hopkins Bloomberg School of Public Health, October 2017), https://www.cahmi.org/projects/adverse-childhood-experiences-aces/.

8. Evie Blad et al., "The School Shootings of 2018: What's Behind the Numbers," *Education Week,* December 19, 2018, https://www.edweek.org/ew/section/multimedia/the-school-shootings-of-2018-whats-behind.html.

9. Schwartz, "Teachers Support Social-Emotional Learning"; Wendy M. Reinke et al., "Supporting Children's Mental Health in Schools: Teacher Perceptions of Needs, Roles, and Barriers," *School Psychology Quarterly* 26, no. 1 (March 2011):1–13, doi:10.1037/a0022714; Heather J. Walter, Karen Gouze, and Karen G. Lim, "Teachers' Beliefs About Mental Health Needs in Inner City Elementary Schools," *Journal of the American Academy of Child and Adolescent Psychiatry* 45, no. 1 (January 2006): 61–68, https://jaacap.org/article/S0890-8567(09)62261-9/fulltext.

10. "Core SEL Competencies," Collaborative for Academic, Social, and Emotional Learning (CASEL), 2019, https://casel.org/core-competencies/.

11. Catherine Raeff, "Independence and Interdependence in Children's Developmental Experiences," *Child Development Perspectives* 4, no. 1. (2010): 31–36, doi:10.1111/j.1750-8606.2009.00113.x; CASEL, "Core SEL Competencies."

12. "Social Emotional Learning Standards," Illinois State Board of Education (website), 2019, https://www.isbe.net/Pages/Social-Emotional-Learning-Standards.aspx; "Social and Emotional Learning (SEL) Standards and Benchmarks for the Anchorage School District," UCLA Center for MH in Schools & Student/Learning Supports, 2019, http://smhp.psych.ucla.edu/pdfdocs/sel%20standards%20and%20benchmarks%20_anchorage%20school%20dist_.pdf.

13. Kim Schonert-Reichl, Jennifer L. Hanson-Peterson, and Shelley Hymel, "SEL and Preservice Teacher Education," in *Handbook of Social and Emotional Learning,* ed. Joseph A. Durlak et al. (New York: Guilford Press, 2015), 406; Bridgeland, Bruce, and Hariharan, *The Missing Piece.*

14. Jennifer DePaoli, Matthew N. Atwell, and John Bridgeland, *Ready to Lead: A National Principal Survey on How Social and Emotional Learning Can Prepare Children and Transform Schools* (Chicago: CASEL, 2017), http://www.casel.org/wp-content/uploads/2017/11/ReadyToLead_FINAL.pdf; Tracy Ehlers, "Supporting Beginning Teachers Through Mentorship" (master's thesis, Concordia University, St. Paul, MN, 2019), https://digitalcommons.csp.edu/cgi/viewcontent.cgi?article=1008&context=teacher-education_masters.

15. Center for Reaching & Teaching the Whole Child, http://crtwc.org/.

CHAPTER 1

1. Rebeca Diaz, *Year 3 Report for Center for Reaching & Teaching the Whole Child* (San Francisco: WestEd, 2017, unpublished report for CRTWC).

2. Geneva Gay, *Culturally Responsive Teaching: Theory, Research, and Practice*, 3rd ed. (New York: Teachers College, 2018); Kris Gutierrez and Joanne Larson, "Discussing Expanded Spaces for Learning," *Language Arts* 85, no. 1 (September 2007), http://hdl.handle.net/1802/23523.

3. Brian Arao and Kristi Clemens, *From Safe to Brave Spaces in the Art of Effective Facilitation* (Sterling, VA: Stylus Publishing, 2013).

4. Sharroky Hollie, *Culturally and Linguistically Responsive Teaching and Learning: Classroom Practices for Student Success,* 2nd ed. (Huntington Beach, CA: Shell Education, 2018).

5. Gay, *Culturally Responsive Teaching*; Gutierrez and Larson, "Discussing Expanded Spaces"; Beverly Tatum, *Why Are All the Black Kids Sitting Together in the Cafeteria?* (New York: Basic Books, 2017); Hollie, *Culturally and Linguistically Responsive Teaching.*

6. Robert J. Jagers, Deborah Rivas-Drake, and Teresa Borowski, *Equity & Social and Emotional Learning: A Cultural Analysis*, Frameworks Briefs (Chicago: CASEL, 2018), https://measuringsel.casel.org/wp-content/uploads/2018/11/Frameworks-Equity.pdf; Aspen Institute Education and Society Program, *Pursuing Social and Emotional Development Through a Racial Equity Lens: A Call to Action* (Washington, DC: Aspen Institute, 2018), https://assets.aspeninstitute.org/content/uploads/2018/05/Aspen-Institute_Framing-Doc_Call-to-Action.pdf.

7. Jagers, Rivas-Drake, and Borowski, *Equity & Social and Emotional Learning*; Aspen Institute, *Pursuing Social and Emotional Development.*

8. Stephanie M. Jones, Suzanne M. Bouffard, and Richard Weissbourd, "Educators' Social and Emotional Skills Vital to Learning," *Phi Delta Kappan* 94, no. 8 (May 2013), 62–65, doi:10.1177/003172171309400815; Joseph E. Zins et al., "The Scientific Base Linking Social and Emotional Learning to School Success," in *Building Academic Success on Social Emotional Learning: What Does the Research Say?*, ed. Joseph E. Zins et al. (New York: Teachers College Press, 2004).

9. Patricia A. Jennings and Mark T. Greenberg, "The Prosocial Classroom: Teacher Social and Emotional Competence in Relation to Student and Classroom Outcomes," *Review of Educational Research* 79 (2009): 491–525, doi:10.3102/0034654308325693; Jones, Bouffard, and Weissbourd, "Educators' Social and Emotional Skills."

10. Urie Bronfenbrenner, *The Ecology of Human Development* (Cambridge, MA: Harvard University Press, 1979).

11. The Aspen Institute Community Roundtable for Change, *Glossary for Understanding the Dismantling Structural Racism/Promoting Racial Equity Analysis* (Washington, DC: Aspen Institute, n.d.), https://assets.aspeninstitute.org/content/uploads/files/content/docs/rcc/RCC-Structural-Racism-Glossary.pdf.

12. Nora Gordon, *Disproportionality in Student Discipline: Connecting Policy to Research* (Washington, DC: Brookings Institution, 2018), https://www.brookings.edu/research/disproportionality-in-student-discipline-connecting-policy-to-research/.

13. Gordon, *Disproportionality in Student Discipline.*

14. Jayanti Owens and Sara S. McLanahan, "Unpacking the Drivers of Racial Disparities in School Suspension and Expulsion," *Social Forces,* June 20, 2019, doi:10.1093/sf/

soz095/5521044; Russell Skiba et al., "Race Is Not Neutral: A National Investigation of African American and Latino Disproportionality in School Discipline," *School Psychology Review* 40, no. 1 (2011), https://www.researchgate.net/publication/267716989_Race_Is_Not_Neutral_A_National_Investigation_of_African_American_and_Latino_Disproportionality_in_School_Discipline.

15. Grover J. Whitehurst, "A Prevalence of Policy-Based Evidence-Making: Forum; Should Schools Embrace Social and Emotional Learning?" *Education Next* 19, no. 3 (Summer 2019), https://www.educationnext.org/prevalence-policy-based-evidence-making-forum-should-schools-embrace-social-emotional-learning/.

16. Aspen Institute National Commission on Social, Emotional, and Academic Development *How Learning Happens: Supporting Students' Social, Emotional, and Academic Learning* (Washington, DC: Aspen Institute, 2017), https://assets.aspeninstitute.org/content/uploads/2018/01/2017_Aspen_InterimReport_Update2.pdf; Kim Schonert-Reichl, Jennifer L. Hanson-Peterson, and Shelley Hymel, "SEL and Preservice Teacher Education," in *Handbook of Social and Emotional Learning*, ed. Joseph A. Durlak et al. (New York: Guilford Press, 2015).

17. National Council on Teacher Quality, *What Makes Teacher Prep "Traditional" or "Non-Traditional?"* (Washington, DC: NCTQ, n.d.), https://www.nctq.org/dmsView/NCTQ_-_What_Makes_Teacher_Prep_Traditional_or_Non_Traditional.

18. Madeline Will, "What Works in Teacher Induction? The New Teacher Center Releases Its Standards," *Education Week*, February 13, 2018, https://blogs.edweek.org/edweek/teacherbeat/2018/02/what_should_teacher_induction_.html.

19. Joseph P. Allen et al., "An Interaction-Based Approach to Enhancing Secondary School Instruction and Student Achievement," *Science* 333, no. 6045 (2011): 1034–1037, doi:10.1126/Science.1207998; Diane Early et al., "Improving Teacher-Child Interactions: A Randomized Controlled Trial of Making the Most of Classroom Interactions and My Teaching Partner Professional Development Models," *Early Childhood Research Quarterly* 38 (2017): 57–70, https://www.sciencedirect.com/science/article/pii/S0885200616300758?via%3Dihub; Sam Portnow, Jason Downer, and Josh Brown, *An Increase in Emotional Support, a Reduction in Negative Social Emotional Skills, or Both? Examining How Universal Social Emotional Programs Achieve Reductions in Aggression* (Evanston, IL: Society for Research on Educational Effectiveness, 2015), https://files.eric.ed.gov/fulltext/ED562106.pdf.

CHAPTER 2

1. Available from the Center for Reaching & Teaching the Whole Child, http://crtwc.org/.

2. Lee S. Shulman, "Signature Pedagogies in the Professions," *Dædalus* 134, no. 3 (Summer 2005): 52–59, doi:10.1162/0011526054622015.

3. Joseph E. Zins et al., "The Scientific Base Linking Social and Emotional Learning to School Success," in *Building Academic Success on Social and Emotional Learning*, ed. Joseph E. Zins et al. (New York: Teachers College Press, 2004), 3–22; National Research Council, *Education for Life and Work: Developing Transferable Knowledge and Skills in the 21st Century* (Washington, DC: National Academies Press, 2012), doi:10.17226/13398; K. Brooke Stafford-Brizard, *Building*

Blocks for Learning: A Framework for Comprehensive Student Development (New York: Turn-aroundforChildren,2016),https://www.turnaroundusa.org/wp-content/uploads/2016/03/Turnaround-for-Children-Building-Blocks-for-Learningx-2.pdf; Linda Darling-Hammond et al., "Science of Learning and Development: Implications for Educational Practice," *Applied Developmental Science* (February 17, 2019): 425–469, doi:10.1080/10888691.2018.1537791.

4. Joel McFarland et al., "Racial/Ethnic Enrollment in Public Schools," in *The Condition of Education,* NCES 2017-104 (Washington, DC: National Center for Educational Statistics, 2017), https://nces.ed.gov/programs/coe/pdf/coe_cge.pdf.

5. Michael L. Hecht and Young JuShin, "Culture and Social and Emotional Competencies" in *Handbook of Social and Emotional Learning,* ed. Joseph A. Durlak, Celene E. Domitrovich, and Thomas P. Gullotta (New York: Guilford Press, 2015).

6. Anthony Bryk and Barbara Schneider, *Trust In Schools: A Core Resource for Improvement* (New York: Russell Sage Foundation, 2002); Valerie von Frank, "Trust Matters–For Educators, Parents, and Students," *Tools for Schools* 14, no. 1 (Fall 2010): 1–3, https://learningforward.org/docs/tools-for-learning-schools/tools9-10.pdf; Jon Saphier, "Voices: Let's Get Specific About How Leaders Can Build Trust," *The Learning Professional* 39, no. 6 (December 2018), https://learningforward.org/journal/december-2018-volume-39-no-6/lets-get-specific-about-how-leaders-can-build-trust/.

7. Craig Wacker and Lynn Olson, *Teacher Mindset: How Educators' Perspectives Shape Student Success* (Washington, DC: Future Ed, Georgetown University, 2019), https://www.future-ed.org/wp-content/uploads/2019/06/Final-report_Teacher-Mindsets.pdf.

8. Elizabeth N. Chapman, Anna Kaatz, and Molly Carnes, "Physicians and Implicit Bias: How Doctors May Unwittingly Perpetuate Health Care Disparities," *Journal of General Internal Medicine* 28, no.11 (November 2013): 1504–10, doi:10.1007/s11606-013-2441-1.

9. Glenn E. Singleton, *Courageous Conversations About Race: A Field Guide for Achieving Equity in Schools* (Thousand Oaks, CA: Corwin Press, 2014).

10. Ilana Umanksy and Hanna Dumont, *English Learner Labeling: How English Learner Status Shapes Teacher Perceptions of Student Skills and the Moderating Role of Bilingual Instructional Settings* (Providence, RI: Brown University Annenberg Institute, 2019), https://edworkingpapers.com/sites/default/files/ai19-94.pdf.

11. Ellen Bialystok, Fergus I. M. Craik, and Gigi Luk, "Bilingualism: Consequences for Mind and Brain," *Trends in Cognitive Sciences* 16, no. 4 (2012): 240–250, doi:10.1016/j.tics.2012.03.001; Yudhijit Bhattacharjee, "The Benefits of Bilingualism," *New York Times,* March 17, 2012, https://www.nytimes.com/2012/03/18/opinion/sunday/the-benefits-of-bilingualism.html.

12. Aida Walqui et al., *What Are We Doing to Middle School English Learners? Findings and Recommendations for Change from a Study of California EL Programs* (Narrative Summary), (San Francisco: WestEd, 2010).

13. Amanda Oleson and Matthew T. Hora, "Teaching the Way They Were Taught? Revisiting the Sources of Teaching Knowledge and the Role of Prior Experience in Shaping Faculty Teaching Practices," *Higher Education* 68, no. 1 (July 2013), doi:10.1007/s10734-013-9678-9; Linda Darling-Hammond and Jeannie Oakes, *Preparing Teachers for Deeper Learning* (Cambridge, MA: Harvard Education Press, 2019), 110–116.

14. Matthew A. Kraft, David Blazar, and Dylan Hogan, "The Effect of Teacher Coaching on Instruction and Achievement: A Meta-Analysis of the Causal Evidence," *Review of Educational Research* 88, no. 4 (2018): 547–588, https://scholar.harvard.edu/files/mkraft/files/kraft_blazar_hogan_2017_teacher_coaching_meta_analysis_wp.pdf.

15. Donald Boyd et al., "Complex by Design: Investigating Pathways into Teaching in New York City Schools," *Journal of Teacher Education* 57 (April 2005): 155–166, doi:10.1177/0022487105285943.

16. Darling-Hammond and Oakes, *Preparing Teachers for Deeper Learning*, 110–116.

17. Anthony S. Bryk et al., *Learning to Improve: How America's Schools Can Get Better at Getting Better* (Cambridge, MA: Harvard Education Press, 2015); Catherine Lewis, "What Is Improvement Science? Do We Need It in Education?" *Educational Researcher* 44, no. 1 (2015): 54–61, http://www.diplomasnow.org/wp-content/uploads/2015/07/what-is-improvement-science.pdf.

18. Collaborative for Academic, Social, and Emotional Learning (CASEL), *Guide: Effective Social and Emotional Learning Programs–Preschool and Elementary School Edition* (Chicago: CASEL, 2013); Camille A. Farrington et al., *Teaching Adolescents to Become Learners: The Role of Noncognitive Factors in Shaping School Performance; A Critical Literature Review* (Chicago: University of Chicago Consortium on Chicago School Research, 2012); Patricia A. Jennings and Mark T. Greenberg, "The Prosocial Classroom: Teacher Social and Emotional Competence in Relation to Student and Classroom Outcomes," *Review of Educational Research* 79 (2009): 491–525, doi:10.3102/0034654308325693; Marc A. Brackett, Nicole A. Elbertson, and Susan E. Rivers, "Applying Theory to the Development of Approaches to SEL," in *Handbook of Social and Emotional Learning*, ed. Joseph A. Durlak et al. (New York: Guilford Press, 2015), 20–32; Carol. S. Dweck, *Mindset: The New Psychology of Success; How We Can Learn to Fulfill Our Potential* (New York: Random House, 2016); Stephanie M. Jones, Suzanne M. Bouffard, and Richard Weissbourd, "Educators' Social and Emotional Skills Vital to Learning." *Phi Delta Kappan* 94, no. 8 (May 2013), 62–65, doi:10.1177/003172171309400815; Geneva Gay, *Culturally Responsive Teaching: Theory, Research, and Practice*, 3rd ed. (New York: Teachers College Press, 2018); Gloria Ladson-Billings, *The Dreamkeepers: Successful Teachers of African American Children* (San Francisco: Jossey-Bass, 2009); Zaretta L. Hammond, *Culturally Responsive Teaching and the Brain: Promoting Authentic Engagement and Rigor Among Culturally and Linguistically Diverse Students* (Thousand Oaks, CA: Corwin Press, 2015).

19. Deborah L. Ball and Francesca Forzani, "Teaching Skillful Teaching," *Educational Leadership* 68, no. 4 (2010): 40–45, https://www.researchgate.net/publication/299130992_Teaching_skillful_teaching; "Work of Teaching," University of Michigan Teachingworks (website), http://www.teachingworks.org/work-of-teaching.

20. "Teacher Moves: Facilitate Student Reasoning and Collaboration," Doing and Talking Math and Science (website), Wisconsin Center for Education Research, School of Education, University of Wisconsin-Madison, http://stem4els.wceruw.org/How/teacher.html.

21. Andrew J. Hill and Daniel B. Jones, "A Teacher Who Knows Me: The Academic Benefits of Repeat Student-Teacher Matches," *Economics of Education Review* 64 (June 2018): 1–12, https://aefpweb.org/sites/default/files/webform/42/HillJones_ATeacherWhoKnowsMe_

March2017.pdf; Robert Pianta, *Enhancing Relationships Between Children and Teachers* (Washington, DC: American Psychological Association, 1999), doi:10.1037/10314-000; Marilyn Watson and Laura Ecken, *Learning to Trust* (New York: Oxford University Press, 2019).

22. Harry K. Wong and Rosemary T. Wong, *The First Days of School: How to Be an Effective Teacher,* 5th ed. (Mountain View, CA: Harry K. Wong Publications, 2019); Todd Whitaker, Madeline Whitaker, and Katherine Whitaker, *Your First Year: How to Survive and Thrive as a New Teacher* (New York: Routledge, 2016); Julia G. Thompson, *The First-Year Teacher's Survival Guide: Ready-to-Use Strategies, Tools and Activities for Meeting the Challenges of Each School Day,* 2nd ed. (San Francisco: Jossey-Bass, 2007); Paula Denton and Roxane Kriete, *The First Six Weeks of School* (Turners Falls, MA: Center for Responsive Schools, 2015).

23. Patricia Jennings, *The Trauma Sensitive Classroom: Building Resilience with Compassionate Teaching* (New York: W.W. Norton, 2018); Watson and Ecken, *Learning to Trust*; Sharroky Hollie, *Culturally and Linguistically Responsive Teaching and Learning: Classroom Practices for Student Success,* 2nd ed. (Huntington Beach, CA: Shell Education, 2018); Judith Kleinfeld, "Positive Stereotyping: The Cultural Relativist in the Classroom," *Human Organization* 34, no. 3 (Fall 1975): 269–274, doi:10.17730/humo.34.3.57815p18h4661010.

24. Watson and Ecken, *Learning to Trust.*

25. Denton and Kriete, *The First Six Weeks of School.*

26. Barbara T. Bowman, "Self-Reflection As an Element of Professionalism," *Teachers College Record* 90, no. 3 (1989): 444–451; Deborah S. Yost, "Reflection and Self-Efficacy: Enhancing the Retention of Qualified Teachers from a Teacher Education Perspective," *Teacher Education Quarterly* 33, no. 4 (2006): 59–76.

27. Leonora G. Weil et al., "The Development of Metacognitive Ability in Adolescence," *Consciousness and Cognition* 22, no. 1 (March 2013), https://www.sciencedirect.com/science/article/pii/S1053810013000068; Zemira R. Mevarech and Chagit Amran, "Immediate and Delayed Effects of Meta-Cognitive Instruction on Regulation of Cognition and Mathematics Achievement," *Metacognition and Learning* 3, no. 2 (2008): 147–157.

28. Arthur L. Costa and Bena Kallick, eds., *Learning and Leading with Habits of Mind: 16 Essential Characteristics for Success* (Alexandria, VA: ASCD, 2008).

29. Lev S. Vygotsky and Michael Cole, *Mind in Society: The Development of Higher Psychological Processes* (Cambridge, MA: Harvard University Press, 1978); Rita Tracy, 2012 PowerPoint slide for her work with high school students.

30. Linda Lantieri, *Building Emotional Intelligence: Practices to Cultivate Inner Resilience in Children* (Boulder, CO: Sounds True, 2008); Patricia Jennings and Daniel Siegel, *Mindfulness for Teachers* (New York: W.W. Norton, 2015).

31. Jill Barshay, "20 Judgments a Teacher Makes in 1 Minute and 28 Seconds," *Hechinger Report,* 2018, https://hechingerreport.org/20-judgments-a-teacher-makes-in-1-minute-and-28-seconds; Patricia G. Devine et al., "Long-Term Reduction in Implicit Race Bias: A Prejudice Habit-Breaking Intervention," *Journal of Experimental Social Psychology* 48, no. 6 (2012): 1267–1278.

32. Singleton, *Courageous Conversations About Race.*

33. Kristen E. Lyons and Philip David Zelazo, "Monitoring, Metacognition, and Executive Function: Elucidating the Role of Self-Reflection in the Development of Self-Regulation,"

Advances in Child Development and Behavior, vol. 40, ed. Janette Benson (Burlington, MA: Elsevier Academic Press, 2011): 379–412, doi:10.1016/B978-0-12-386491-8.00010-4.

34. Dweck, *Mindset.*

35. Dweck, *Mindset.*

36. Gail L. Sunderman, James S. Kim, and Gary Orfield, *NCLB Meets School Realities: Lessons from the Field* (Thousand Oaks, CA: Corwin Press, 2005).

37. Angela Duckworth, *Grit: The Power of Passion and Perseverance* (New York: Scribner, 2016); Marcus Credé, Michael C. Tynan, and Peter D. Harms, "Much Ado About Grit: A Meta-Analytic Synthesis of the Grit Literature," *Journal of Personality and Social Psychology* 113, no. 3 (2017): 492; Marcus Credé, "What Shall We Do about Grit? A Critical Review of What We Know and What We Don't Know," *Educational Researcher* 47, no. 9 (2018): 606–611; Katherine Muenks, Ji Seung Yang, and Allan Wigfield, "Associations Between Grit, Motivation, and Achievement in High School Students," *Motivation Science* 4, no. 2 (2018): 158.

38. Credé, Tynan, and Harms, "Much Ado About Grit."

39. Doug M. Clarke and Barbara A. Clarke, "Encouraging Perseverance in Elementary Mathematics: A Tale of Two Problems," *Teaching Children Mathematics* 10, no. 4 (2003): 204–209; Watson and Ecken, *Learning to Trust.*

40. Regan Aymett and Kevin S. Krahenbuhl, "Teaching Goal Setting to Help Students Take Ownership of Learning," *ASCD Express* 12, no. 1 (2016), http://www.ascd.org/ascd-express/vol12/1201-aymett.aspx.

41. Sunderman, Kim, and Orfield, *NCLB Meets School Realities.*

42. Amrit Thapa et al., "A Review of School Climate Research," *Review of Educational Research* 83, no. 3 (2013): 357–385, https://education.ucdavis.edu/sites/main/files/file-attachments/thapa_cohen_guffey_and_higgins-dallesandro_2013.pdf.

43. Linda Darling-Hammond and Channa Cook-Harvey, *Educating the Whole Child: Improving School Climate to Support Student Success* (Palo Alto, CA: Learning Policy Institute, 2018), https://learningpolicyinstitute.org/sites/default/files/product-files/Educating_Whole_Child_REPORT.pdf; Watson and Ecken, *Learning to Trust.*

44. "The Glossary of Educational Reform," Great Schools Partnership (website), 2014, https://www.edglossary.org/

45. Karen F. Osterman, "Students' Need for Belonging in the School Community," *Review of Educational Research* 70, no. 3 (September 2000): 323–367, doi:10.3102/00346543070003323.

46. Elizabeth G. Cohen et al., "Complex Instruction: Equity in Cooperative Learning Classrooms," *Theory into Practice* 38, no. 2 (March 1999): 80–86, doi:10.1080/00405849909543836.

47. Elizabeth Cohen and Rachel Lotan, *Designing Groupwork: Strategies for the Heterogeneous Classroom* (New York: Teachers College Press, 2014).

48. Shane R. Jimerson, Emily Campos, and Jennifer L. Greif, "Toward an Understanding of Definitions and Measures of School Engagement and Related Terms," *The California School Psychologist* 8, no. 1 (2003): 7–27, doi:10.1007/BF03340893.

49. Jennifer Fredricks, Phyllis C. Blumenfeld, and Alison H. Paris, "School Engagement: Potential of the Concept, State of the Evidence," *Review of Educational Research* 74, no. 1 (2004): 59–109,

http://www.inquirylearningcenter.org/wp-content/uploads/2015/08/Fredricks2004-engagemt.pdf.

50. Gay, *Culturally Responsive Teaching*; Hammond, *Culturally Responsive Teaching and the Brain.*

51. Sharroky Hollie, *Culturally and Linguistically Responsive Teaching and Learning: Classroom Practices for Student Success,* 2nd edition (Huntington Beach, CA: Shell Education, 2017); Geneva Gay, "Connections between Classroom Management and Culturally Responsive Teaching," in *Handbook of Classroom Management: Research, Practice, and Contemporary Issues,* ed. Carolyn M. Evertson and Carol S. Weinstein (Mahwah, NJ: Lawrence Erlbaum Associates, 2006), 343-370; Zaretta Hammond, *Culturally Responsive Teaching and the Brain: Promoting Authentic Engagement and Rigor among Culturally and Linguistically Diverse Students* (Thousand Oaks, CA: Corwin Press, 2014).

52. Robyn Gillies, "Cooperative Learning: Review of Research and Practice," *Australian Journal of Teacher Education* 41, no. 3 (2016): 39–51, doi:10.14221/ajte.2016v41n3.3; David Johnson and Frank Johnson, *Joining Together: Group Theory and Group Skills,* 10th ed. (Upper Saddle River, N.J: Pearson Education, 2009).

53. Hammond, *Culturally Responsive Teaching and the Brain.*

54. Eva Kyndt et al., "A Meta-Analysis of the Effects of Face-to-Face Cooperative Learning: Do Recent Studies Falsify or Verify Earlier Findings?" *Educational Research Review* 10 (2013): 133–149, https://www.sciencedirect.com/science/article/pii/S1747938X13000122?via%3Dihub.

55. Jeff Zwiers and Marie Crawford, *Academic Conversations: Classroom Talk That Fosters Critical Thinking and Content Understandings* (Portland, Maine: Stenhouse Publishers, 2011).

56. US Department of Education, *Our Nation's English Learners* (2017), https://www2.ed.gov/datastory/el-characteristics/index.html

57. Claude M. Steele, *Whistling Vivaldi and Other Clues to How Stereotypes Affect Us* (New York: W.W. Norton, 2010); Hammond, *Culturally Responsive Teaching and the Brain.*

58. Ross W. Greene and J. Stuart Ablon, *Treating Explosive Kids: The Collaborative Problem-Solving Approach* (New York: Guilford Press, 2005).

59. Derald Wing Sue, *Microaggressions in Everyday Life: Race, Gender, and Sexual Orientation* (Hoboken, NJ: Wiley, 2010); Watson and Ecken, *Learning to Trust*; Brenda Morrison, Peta Blood, and Margaret Thorsborne, "Practicing Restorative Justice in School Communities: The Challenge of Culture Change," *Public Organization Review: A Global Journal* 5 (2005): 335–357; Jessica Minahan and Nancy Rappaport, *The Behavior Code: A Practical Guide to Understanding and Teaching the Most Challenging Students* (Cambridge, MA: Harvard Education Press, 2012).

60. Roland G. Fryer, "Acting White: The Social Price Paid by the Best and Brightest Minority Students," *Education Next.* 6, no. 1 (Winter 2006), https://www.educationnext.org/actingwhite/.

CHAPTER 3

1. "Lesson One: Introduction–Mindful Bodies and Listening," Mindful Schools (website), https://e7n7r7a7.stackpathcdn.com/wp/wp-content/uploads/2015/06/starter-lesson.pdf.

2. Kate Sciandia, *The Mindfulness Habit: Six Weeks to Creating the Habit of Being Present* (Woodbury, MN: Llewellyn, 2015); Jon Kabat-Zinn, "Mindfulness-Based Interventions in Context: Past, Present, and Future," *Clinical Psychology: Science and Practice* 10, no. 2 (2003): 144–156, http://institutpsychoneuro.com/wp-content/uploads/2015/09/Kabat-Zinn-2003.pdf.

3. Tim Myers, *Basho and the Fox* (New York: Cavendish Square Publishing, 2000).

4. California Department of Education (2010), https://www.cde.ca.gov/re/cc/whatareccss.asp.

5. Roxanne Kriete and Carol Davis, *The Morning Meeting Book,* 3rd ed. (Turners Falls, MA: Northeast Foundation for Children, 2014).

6. Yangsook Choi, *The Name Jar* (New York: Random House, 2003).

7. Jacqueline Woodson, *The Day You Begin* (New York: Penguin Random House, 2018); Alexandra Penfold and Suzanne Kaufman, *All Are Welcome* (New York: Penguin Random House, 2018).

8. Kim Schonert-Reichl et al. "Enhancing Cognitive and Social–Emotional Development Through a Simple-to-Administer Mindfulness-Based School Program for Elementary School Children: A Randomized Controlled Trial," *Developmental Psychology* 51, no. 1 (2015): 52–66, doi:10.1037/a0038454; Patricia A. Jennings et al., "Improving Classroom Learning Environments by Cultivating Awareness and Resilience in Education (CARE): Results of a Randomized Controlled Trial," *School Psychology Quarterly* 28, no. 4 (2013), 374–390, https://psycnet.apa.org/doiLanding?doi=10.1037%2Fspq0000035.

9. JoAnn Deak, *Your Fantastic Elastic Brain* (Naperville, IL: Sourcebooks, 2017).

10. Judy Willis, "From Math Negative to Math Positive Attitudes in Your Kids," *Psychology Today* (blog), March 15, 2016, https://www.psychologytoday.com/us/blog/radical-teaching/201603/math-negative-math-positive-attitudes-in-your-kids.

11. California State Board of Education, California Common Core State Standards (2013), https://www.cde.ca.gov/be/st/ss/documents/finalclaccssstandards.pdf.

12. "10 Reasons Why Having a Lesson Plan Is Important," *EdSys* (blog), April 25, 2018, https://www.edsys.in/10-reasons-lesson-plan-important/.

CHAPTER 4

1. Kim Schonert-Reichl, Jennifer L. Hanson-Peterson, and Shelley Hymel, "SEL and Preservice Teacher Education" in *Handbook of Social and Emotional Learning,* ed. Joseph A. Durlak et al. (New York: Guilford Press, 2015).

2. Linda Darling-Hammond and Jeannie Oakes, eds., *Preparing Teachers for Deeper Learning* (Cambridge, MA: Harvard Education Press, 2019); Steven Z. Athanases and Luciana C. de Oliveira, "Advocacy for Equity in Classrooms and Beyond: New Teachers' Challenges and Responses," *Teachers College Record* 110, no. 1 (2008): 64–104, https://eric.ed.gov/?id=EJ825484; Gloria Ladson-Billings, *Crossing Over to Canaan: The Journey of New Teachers in Diverse Classrooms* (San Francisco: Jossey-Bass, 2001).

3. Athanases and de Oliveira, "Advocacy for Equity in Classrooms and Beyond."

4. John Bridgeland, Mary Bruce, and Arya Hariharan, *The Missing Piece: A National Teacher Survey on How Social and Emotional Learning Can Empower Children and Transform*

Schools. A Report for CASEL (Chicago: CASEL, 2016), https://casel.org/wp-content/uploads/2016/01/the-missing-piece.pdf; James R. Koller et al., "Differences Between Novice and Expert Teachers' Undergraduate Preparation and Ratings of Importance in the Area of Children's Mental Health," *International Journal of Mental Health Promotion* 6 (2004): 40–45, doi:10.1080/14623730.2004.9721930; Coalition for Psychology in Schools and Education, *Report on the Teacher Needs Survey* (Washington, DC: American Psychological Association, Center of Psychology in Schools, August 2006), https://www.apa.org/ed/schools/coalition/teachers-needs.pdf; Stephanie M. Jones and Suzanne M. Bouffard, "Social and Emotional Learning in Schools: From Programs to Strategies," *Social Policy Report* 26, no. 4 (2012): 1–22.

5. Jennifer L. Snow-Gerono, "Professional Development in a Culture of Inquiry: PDS Teachers Identify the Benefits of Professional Learning Communities," *Teaching and Teacher Education* 21, no. 3 (2005): 241–256; Lynne Cavazos, "Forms and Functions of Teacher Talk," in *Talking Shop: Authentic Conversation and Teacher Learning*, ed. Christopher M. Clark (New York: Teachers College Press, 2001): 137–171.

6. Jinfa Cai and F. Joseph Merlino, "Metaphor: A Powerful Means for Assessing Students' Mathematical Disposition," in *Motivation and Disposition: Pathways to Learning Mathematics*, ed. Daniel J. Brahier and William Speer (Reston, VA: National Council of Teachers of Mathematics, 2011): 147–156.

7. Patricia E. Swanson, "Overcoming the 'Run' Response," *Mathematics Teaching in the Middle School* 19, no. 2 (September 2013): 94–99, https://eric.ed.gov/?id=EJ1029397.

8. Ron Larson et al., *McDougal Littell Math Course 1* (Evanston, IL: McDougal Littell, 2008), 263.

9. Louise Derman-Sparks, "Guide for Selecting Anti-Bias Children's Books," Teaching for Change (website), April 14, 2016, https://www.teachingforchange.org/selecting-anti-bias-books.

10. Zaretta L. Hammond, *Culturally Responsive Teaching and the Brain: Promoting Authentic Engagement and Rigor Among Culturally and Linguistically Diverse Students* (Thousand Oaks, CA: Corwin Press, 2015); Elizabeth Bridges Smith, "Anchored in Our Literature: Students Responding to African American Literature," *Language Arts* 72, no. 8 (1995), 571–574; Kathryn Au, *Multicultural Issues and Literacy Achievement* (Abingdon, UK: Routledge, 2013); Delmae Darling, "Improving Minority Student Achievement by Making Cultural Connections," *Middle School Journal* 36, no. 5 (2005): 46–50.

11. Edward L. Deci, Richard Koestner, and Richard Ryan, "A Meta-Analytic Review of Experiments Examining the Effects of Extrinsic Rewards on Intrinsic Motivation," *Psychological Bulletin* 125, no. 6 (November 1999): 627–668, https://psycnet.apa.org/buy/1999-01567-001.

12. Mandy Savitz-Romer and Suzanne Bouffard, *Ready, Willing, and Able: A Developmental Approach to College Access and Success* (Cambridge, MA: Harvard Education Press, 2012).

13. Amy Cyphert, "Addressing Racial Disparities in Preschool Suspension and Expulsion Rates," *Tennessee Law Review* 82 (2015), https://papers.ssrn.com/sol3/papers.cfm?abstract_id=3264109.

14. Joanne Golann and Mira Debs, "The Harsh Discipline of No-Excuses Charter Schools: Is It Worth the Promise?," *Education Week* 38, no. 36 (June 9, 2019): 20, https://www.edweek.org/ew/articles/2019/06/09/the-harsh-discipline-of-no-excuses-charter-schools.html.

15. Joanne W. Golann, Mira Debs, and Anna Lisa Weiss, "'To Be Strict on Your Own': Black and Latinx Parents Evaluate Discipline in Urban Choice Schools," *American Educational Research Journal*, (March 7, 2019), doi:10.3102/0002831219831972.

16. Savitz-Romer and Bouffard, *Ready, Willing, and Able.*

17. Jal Mehta and Sarah Fine, *In Search of Deeper Learning: The Quest to Remake the American High School* (Cambridge, MA: Harvard University Press, 2019); Arianna Prothero and Alex Harwin, "In Many Charter High Schools, Graduation Odds Are Slim," *Education Week* 38, no. 23 (February 26, 2019): 1, https://www.edweek.org/ew/articles/2019/02/27/in-many-charter-high-schools-graduation-odds.html; KIPP, *The Promise of College Completion: KIPP's Early Successes and Challenges* (San Francisco: KIPP Foundation, 2016), http://www.kipp.org/wp-content/uploads/2016/09/CollegeCompletionReport.pdf.

18. Golann, Debs, and Weiss, "To Be Strict on Your Own."

19. National School Reform Faculty, *Looking at Student Work: Student Work Analysis Protocol* (Maplewood, MN: Harmony Education Center, 2015), https://www.nsrfharmony.org/wp-content/uploads/2017/10/StudentWorkAnalysis_0.pdf.

20. Allen N. Mendler, *When Teaching Gets Tough: Smart Ways to Reclaim Your Game* (Alexandria, VA: ASCD, 2012).

21. Jorge Ballinas, "Where Are You From and Why Are You Here? Microaggressions, Racialization, and Mexican College Students in a New Destination," *Sociological Inquiry* 87, no. 2 (May 2017): 385–410, https://onlinelibrary.wiley.com/toc/1475682x/2017/87/2.

22. Suzanne Bouffard, "Social and Emotional Learning in Teacher Education: Where We Are and Where Do We Need to Go?" (unpublished case study for CRTWC, 2018).

23. Linda Darling-Hammond and Jeannie Oakes, *Preparing Teachers for Deeper Learning* (Cambridge, MA: Harvard Education Press, 2019).

24. Mary Hatwood Futrell et al., "The Value of Field Experience and Mentoring in Teacher Preparation: Views from the Experts," Edutopia (website), January 29, 2007, https://www.edutopia.org/value-field-experience-and-mentoring-teacher-preparation.

CHAPTER 5

1. Learning Forward, *Standards for Professional Learning: Facilitator's Guide* (Dallas, TX: Learning Forward, 2011), https://www.learningforward.org/docs/default-source/pdf/facilitatorguide.pdf.

2. "SEL Support & Resources," Austin Independent School District (website), 2018, https://www.austinisd.org/sel/resources.

3. "SEL Community," Anchorage School District (website), 2019, https://www.asdk12.org/Page/6646; "Social Emotional Learning (SEL)," North East Independent School District, San Antonio (website), https://www.neisd.net/Page/20111; "Social Emotional Learning: Meet the Team," Atlanta Public School District (website), https://www.atlantapublicschools.us/Page/53075; CASEL, *Key Insights from the Collaborating Districts Initiative* (Chicago: CASEL, March 2017), https://www.casel.org/wp-content/uploads/2017/03/Final-CDI-Report-3-17-17.pdf.

4. Amuhelang Magaya and Thomas Crawley, "The Perceptions of School Administrators on the Selection Criteria and Training of Cooperating Teachers; Strategies to Foster Collaboration

Between Universities Public Schools," *International Journal of Educational Leadership Preparation* 6, no. 2 (April–June 2011), https://eric.ed.gov/?id=EJ973837.

5. Rebeca Diaz, *Evaluation of the CRTWC Program at San Jose State University: Year 1* (San Francisco: WestEd, 2014, unpublished report for CRTWC).

6. Ellen Meyers, "Keeping New Teachers from Dropping Out," *Gotham Gazette*, February 20, 2006, https://www.gothamgazette.com/index.php/state/3162-keeping-new-teachers-from-dropping-out.

7. From Melanie Miller, M.Ed., activity adjusted from work by Lynn Puteran, NLP-Manitoba

8. Jianping Sheng, "Teacher Retention and Attrition in Public Schools: Evidence from SASS91," *The Journal of Educational Research* 91, no. 2 (1997): 81–88, doi:10.1080/00220679709597525; Heather G. Peske et al., "The Next Generation of Teachers: Changing Conceptions of a Career in Teaching," *Phi Delta Kappan* 83, no. 4 (2001): 304–11, doi:10.1177/003172170108300409; Susan Moore Johnson, *The Workplace Matters: Teacher Quality, Retention, and Effectiveness* (Washington, DC: National Educational Association, 2006), https://files.eric.ed.gov/fulltext/ED495822.pdf.

9. Brian Arao and Kristi Clemens, "From Safe Spaces to Brave Spaces: A New Way to Frame Dialogue Around Diversity and Social Justice," in *The Art of Effective Facilitation,* ed. Lisa M. Landreman (Sterling, VA: Stylus Publishing, 2013).

10. Russell J. Skiba et al., "The Color of Discipline: Sources of Racial and Gender Disproportionality in School Punishment," *The Urban Review* 34, no. 4 (December 2002): 317–342, doi:10.1023/A:1021320817372; Edward Morris and Brea L. Perry, "The Punishment Gap: School Suspensions and Racial Disparities in Achievement," *Social Problems* 63 (2016): 68–86, doi:10.1093/socpro/spv026.

11. US Department of Education Office for Civil Rights, *Data Snapshot: School Discipline,* Issue Brief No. 1 (Washington, DC: US Department of Education, March 2014), https://files.eric.ed.gov/fulltext/ED577231.pdf; Walter S. Gilliam et al., *Do Early Educators' Implicit Biases Regarding Sex and Race Relate to Behavior Expectations and Recommendations of Preschool Expulsions and Suspensions?* (New Haven, CT: Yale Child Study Center, 2016), https://medicine.yale.edu/childstudy/zigler/publications/Preschool%20Implicit%20Bias%20Policy%20Brief_final_9_26_276766_5379_v1.pdf.

12. Gilliam et al., *Early Educators' Implicit Biases.*

13. Yolanda Anyon et al., "The Persistent Effect of Race and the Promise of Alternatives to Suspension in School Discipline Outcomes," *Child and Youth Services Review* 44 (2014): 379–386, https://portal.ct.gov/-/media/SDE/Discipline/Persistent_Effect.pdf.

14. Paul Sperry, "How Liberal Discipline Policies Are Making Schools Less Safe," *New York Post*, March 14, 2015, https://nypost.com/2015/03/14/politicians-are-making-schools-less-safe-and-ruining-education-for-everyone/; Anya Kamenetz and Jessica Bakeman, "Making Schools Safer: Harsh Consequences or Second Chances?" *NPR Ed* (blog), June 22, 2018, https://www.npr.org/sections/ed/2018/06/22/622217666/making-schools-safer-harsh-consequences-or-second-chances.

15. Jessica Minahan and Nancy Rappaport, *The Behavior Code* (Cambridge, MA: Harvard Education Press, 2012).

16. Joseph A. Durlak and Roger P. Weissberg, *The Impact of After-School Programs That Promote Personal and Social Skills*, Executive Summary (Chicago: CASEL, 2007), https://casel .org/wp-content/uploads/2016/08/PDF-1-the-impact-of-after-school-programs-that-promote-personal-and-social-skills-executive-summary.pdf; Jacqueline E. Maloney et al., "A Mindfulness-Based Social and Emotional Learning Curriculum for School-Aged Children: The MindUP Program," in *Handbook of Mindfulness in Education: Integrating Theory and Research into Practice*, ed. Kimberly Schonert-Reichl and Robert Roeser (New York: Springer, 2016), https://link.springer.com/book/10.1007%2F978-1-4939-3506-2; Marc A. Brackett et al., "Enhancing Academic Performance and Social and Emotional Competence with the RULER Feeling Words Curriculum," *Learning and Individual Differences* 22 (2012): 218–224, doi:10.1016/j.lindif.2010.10.002; "PATHS (Promoting Alternative THinking Strategies) Fact Sheet," Pennsylvania State University Evidence-Based Prevention & Intervention Support (EPIS) Center, April 11, 2017, http://www.episcenter.psu.edu/sites/default/files/PATHS_FAQs%204.25.17.pdf; "The 4Rs Program," Morningside Center for Teaching Social Responsibility (website), 2019, https://www.morningsidecenter.org/4rs-program.

17. Joseph A. Durlak et al, "The Impact of Enhancing Student Social and Emotional Learning: A Meta-Analysis of School-Based Universal Interventions," *Child Development* 82, no. 1 (January/February 2001): 405–432, doi:10.1111/j.1467-8624.2010.01564.x.

18. Stephen Burke, "What Teachers Need Most in 2018 (in Every Grade Level and Subject)," *The Donors Choose Blog*, August 6, 2018, https://www.donorschoose.org/blog/what-teachers-need-most-2018/; Sarah Schwartz, "Social-Emotional Learning, Furniture, and Books: What Products Teachers Want Most," *Edweek Market Brief*, Jan 24, 2019, https://marketbrief .edweek.org/marketplace-k-12/donors-choose-2018-survey/?cmp=eml-enl-eu-news2&M =58733118&U=1146925&UUID=6a5558f81b4efcd5a7556bd91c679125.

19. Joseph A. Durlak and Emily P. DuPre, "Implementation Matters: A Review of Research on the Influence of Implementation on Program Outcomes and the Factors Affecting Implementation," *American Journal of Community Psychology* 41, no. 3–4 (2008): 327–350; Stephanie M. Jones et al., *Preparing for Effective SEL Implementation* (New York: Wallace Foundation, 2018), https://www.wallacefoundation.org/knowledge-center/Documents/Preparing-for-Effective-SEL-Implementation.pdf.

CHAPTER 6

1. Curtis W. Linton and Bonnie M. Davis, *Equity 101: Culture* (Thousand Oaks, CA: Corwin Press, 2013).

2. Linda Dusenbury and Roger P. Weissberg, *Emerging Insights from States' Efforts to Strengthen Social and Emotional Learning* (Chicago: CASEL, 2018), https://casel.org/wp-content/uploads/2018/06/CSI-Insights.pdf; Kimberly Kendziora and Nick Yoder, *When Districts Support and Integrate Social and Emotional Learning (SEL): Findings from an Ongoing Evaluation of Districtwide Implementation of SEL* (Washington, DC: Education Policy Center at American Institutes for Research, 2016), https://www.air.org/sites/default/files/downloads/report/When-Districts-Support-and-Integrate-SEL-October-2016.pdf; Hanna Melnick and Lorea Martinez, *Preparing Teachers to Support Social and Emotional Learning: A Case*

Study of San Jose State University and Lakewood Elementary School (Palo Alto, CA: Learning Policy Institute, 2019), https://learningpolicyinstitute.org/sites/default/files/product-files/SEL_CaseStudies_SJSU_Lakewood_REPORT.pdf; Linda Min, "Teacher Educator Institute Cohort Two Final Report" (unpublished report for CRTWC, July 2019); Linda Min, "Teacher Educator Institute Cohort One Follow-Up Report" (unpublished report for CRTWC, July 2019); Suzanne Bouffard, "Developing the Whole Teacher to Educate the Whole Child: Fostering a Social, Emotional, and Cultural Lens Through the Teacher Educator Institute" (unpublished report for CRTWC, July 2018).

3. California Commission on Teacher Credentialing, *California Teaching Performance Expectations (TPEs) Adopted June 2016* (Sacramento, CA: Commission on Teacher Credentialing, 2016), https://www.ctc.ca.gov/docs/default-source/educator-prep/standards/adopted-tpes-2016.pdf.

4. Linda Dusenbury et al., "The Case for Preschool Through High School State Learning Standards for SEL" in *Handbook of Social and Emotional Learning: Research and Practice,* ed. Joseph A. Durlak et al. (New York: Guilford Press, 2015): 532–548.

5. Linda Dusenbury, Caitlin Dermody, and Roger P. Weissberg, *2018 State Scorecard Scan: More States Are Supporting Social and Emotional Learning* (Chicago: CASEL, 2018), https://casel.org/wp-content/uploads/2018/02/2018-State-Scan-FINAL.pdf.

6. Dusenbury, Dermody, and Weissberg, *2018 State Scorecard Scan.*

7. "Social and Emotional Learning," California Department of Education (website), https://www.cde.ca.gov/eo/in/socialemotionallearning.asp.

8. James Cressey, "Social-Emotional Learning in Teacher Education: A Needs Assessment Survey of Teacher Educators" (unpublished report for Massachusetts Consortium for Teacher Educators, 2017).

9. Suzanne Bouffard, "Social and Emotional Learning and Cultural Competence in Teacher Education: Where Are We and Where Do We Need To Go?" (unpublished report for CRTWC, 2018).

10. CASEL, *Key Implementation Insights from the Collaborating Districts Initiative* (Chicago: CASEL, 2017), https://www.casel.org/wp-content/uploads/2017/03/Final-CDI-Report-3-17-17.pdf.

11. CASEL, *Key Implementation Insights,* 8.

12. Kendziora and Yoder, *When Districts Support and Integrate.*

13. David Osher and Kimberly Kendziora, *CASEL/NoVo Collaborating Districts Initiative: Cross-District Outcome Evaluation Report; Executive Summary* (Washington, DC: American Institutes for Research, 2015), 1–5, https://www.casel.org/wp-content/uploads/2016/09/CDI-evaluation-outcomes-report-exec-summary-9-29-16.pdf; Kendziora and Yoder, *When Districts Support and Integrate Social and Emotional Learning (SEL).*

14. See https://casel.org/partner-districts/anchorage-school-district/; https://casel.org/partner-districts/austin-independent-school-district/; https://casel.org/partner-districts/chicago-public-schools/; https://casel.org/partner-districts/cleveland-metropolitan-school-district/; https://casel.org/partner-districts/oakland-unified-school-district/; https://casel.org/partner-districts/metropolitan-nashville-public-schools/.

15. See https://casel.org/partner-districts/chicago-public-schools/.

16. See https://casel.org/partner-districts/chicago-public-schools/; https://casel.org/partner-districts/cleveland-metropolitan-school-district/; https://casel.org/partner-districts/anchorage-school-district/.

17. "Improvement Communities," CORE Districts (website), 2017, https://coredistricts.org/our-work/improvement-communities/; Joel Knudson and Mark Garibaldi, *None of Us Are As Good As All of Us: Early Lessons from the CORE Districts* (San Mateo, CA: American Institutes for Research, 2015), http://coredistricts.org/wp-content/uploads/2017/08/AIR-Report-August-2015.pdf.

18. Suzanne Bouffard, "Making School a Calmer Place to Learn: Schools Integrate Daily Routines for Social-Emotional Learning with Academics," *Harvard Education Letter* 30, no. 1 (January/February 2014): 1–6, http://adventurestoawesome.com/wp-content/uploads/2015/08/Making-School-a-Calmer-Place-to-Learn.pdf.

19. Suzanne Bouffard, "The Moral Imperative of Social and Emotional Learning: Q&A with Meria Carstarphen," *The Learning Professional* 39, no. 4 (August 2018): 22–25, https://learningforward.org/wp-content/uploads/2018/08/the-learning-professional-august-2018.pdf.

20. Bouffard, "Moral Imperative."

21. "Welcome to the Sunnyvale School District: Who We Are," Sunnyvale School District (website), 2019, https://www.sesd.org/domain/295.

22. Sacramento City Unified School District, *Student Study Team Best Practices Manual* (Sacramento, CA: SCUSD, 2015), https://www.scusd.edu/sites/main/files/file-attachments/sst_best_practices_manual_0.pdf.

23. Nancy Markowitz, Wendy Thowdis, and Michael Gallagher, "Sowing Seeds of SEL: University-District Partnership Builds Social and Emotional Learning Across the Teacher Pipeline," *The Learning Professional* 39, no. 4 (August 2018): 30–35, https://learningforward.org/wp-content/uploads/2018/08/the-learning-professional-august-2018.pdf; Patricia Swanson et al., "Trust Your Team: Our Journey to Embed Social and Emotional Learning in a Teacher Education Program Focused on Social Justice," *Teacher Education Quarterly* 46, no. 4 (Fall 2019): 64–88; Deborah Donahue-Keegan, Eleonora Vellegas-Reimers, and James M. Cressey, "Integrating Social-Emotional Learning and Culturally Responsive Teaching in Teacher Education Preparation Programs: The Massachusetts Experience So Far," *Teacher Education Quarterly* 46, no. 4 (Fall 2019): 147; Rochonda L. Nenonene et al., "Challenges and Opportunities in Infusing Social, Emotional, and Cultural Competencies into Teacher Preparation: Our Program's Story," *Teacher Education Quarterly* 46, no. 4 (Fall 2019): 89–112.

24. Based on discussion and feedback from the chair of the SJSU Teacher Education Department.

25. Freeman A. Hrabowski III and Mavis G. Sanders, "Increasing Racial Diversity in the Teacher Workforce: One University's Approach," *Thought & Action* (Winter 2015): 101–116, https://eric.ed.gov/?id=EJ1086971; "The Educator Diversity Gap," Branch Alliance for Educator Diversity (website), https://www.educatordiversity.org/evidence/#educator-gap; Richard Ingersoll and Henry May, *Minority Teacher Recruitment, Employment and Retention: 1987 to 2013* (Palo Alto, CA: Learning Policy Institute, 2016); Richard Ingersoll, "What Do the

National Data Tell Us About Minority Teacher Shortages?," in *The State of Teacher Diversity in American Education* (Washington, DC: Albert Shanker Institute, 2015), https://repository.upenn.edu/gse_pubs/541/.

26. *The State of Teacher Diversity in American Education* (Washington, DC: Albert Shanker Institute, 2015), http://www.shankerinstitute.org/resource/teacherdiversity.

CHAPTER 7

1. Stephanie Levin and Kathryn Bradley, *Understanding and Addressing Principal Turnover: A Review of the Research* (Reston, VA: National Association of Secondary School Principals, 2019), https://learningpolicyinstitute.org/product/nassp-understanding-addressing-principal-turnover-review-research-report; Desiree Carver-Thomas and Linda Darling-Hammond, *Teacher Turnover: Why It Matters and What We Can Do About It* (Palo Alto, CA: Learning Policy Institute, 2017), https://learningpolicyinstitute.org/sites/default/files/product-files/Teacher_Turnover_REPORT.pdf; Gerald L. Natkin et al., "Predicting and Modeling Superintendent Turnover," *Journal of School Leadership* 13, no. 3 (2003): 328–346, doi:10.1177/105268460301300305; John Merrow, *Addicted To Reform: A 12-Step Program to Rescue Public Education* (New York: The New Press, 2017).

Acknowledgments

TEACHING AND LEARNING are fundamentally about relationships and collaboration, as was the process of developing and writing this book. Our thinking about teaching and learning with a social, emotional, and cultural lens has evolved with the insights and experiences of many wonderful colleagues, field leaders, and educators.

The framework at the heart of this book grew out of many years of working to embed social and emotional learning and culturally responsive teaching in teacher education at San José State University. That work was initially encouraged and supported by Dr. Carolyn Nelson, when she was chair of the SJSU Teacher Education Department, and Dean Susan Meyers, former dean of the Connie L. Lurie College of Education. They provided the funding, time, and moral support to create the Center for Reaching & Teaching the Whole Child, which became the incubator for work both within and beyond the university. When SEL was barely on the radar in teacher education, several SJSU faculty members and field supervisors became courageous scouts and jumped into the work with curiosity, openness, and commitment to learn; thank you, in particular, to Patricia Swanson, Colette Rabin, Grinell Smith, Elba Maldonado-Colon, Dale Mitchell, David Whitenack, Mark Felton, Allison Briceno,

Dena Sexton, Jolynn Asato, Roxana Marachi, Lara Kassab, Bonnie Jacobsen, and Marianne Mehuys. As we developed our approach, the CRTWC Advisory Board members provided much-needed feedback, particularly related to the need to address culturally responsive teaching practices. Lisa Medoff, then working at Acknowledge Alliance, also provided valuable insights that helped us bridge the gap between SEL skills and their connection to the academic curriculum in the early stages of our work.

Sunnyvale School District, an informal "lab district" for SJSU and CRTWC, provided path-breaking leadership in social and emotional learning and years of on-the-ground opportunities to develop and refine the anchor competencies framework and the professional learning to implement it. Dr. Michael Gallagher, the visionary district deputy superintendent, gave us the space and opportunity to try out our work with teachers and administrators. Not enough can be said about the Sunnyvale educators who hosted SJSU teacher candidates in their classrooms and schools and attended our workshops. Their perspectives, questions, and ideas were essential to the development of this work. In particular, teachers Rachel Bacosa, Ashley Bondi, Jennifer Concepcion, Lindsay Jacobson, Barbara Papamarcos, Allyson Guida, and principal Pamela Cheng provided an unfailing willingness to give of their time and expertise.

Wendy Thowdis, CRTWC assistant director, has been an invaluable contributor to this book, the framework contained within it, and the work of the center as a whole. Her dedication to thoughtfully refining the work, attention to detail, excellent facilitation skills, and great sense of humor have been essential to whatever we have accomplished. Nance Kwan, CRTWC's operations manager, holds it all together. She spent many hours diligently preparing the manuscript and answering urgent questions, under significant time pressure, all the while maintaining a calmness and grace which we so appreciated.

We are grateful to Nancy Walser, our editor at the Harvard Education Press, for championing this project, for her encouraging way of nudging us and keeping us on track, and for helping us through the weeds. The complexity of integrating the components of social and emotional learning and culturally responsive teaching is part of the value of this work but also an enormous and humbling challenge. Nancy's unfailing ability to sort out the tangles and find the thread is a rare gift. We also extend our thanks to her colleagues at Harvard Education Press, including Laura Cutone Godwin, Rose Ann Miller, Sumita Mukherji, and Katherine Isaacs.

Our thinking and day-to-day work have been shaped by the many researchers, scholars, and organizations cited in the book. We are particularly thankful for the work of CASEL, Linda Darling-Hammond and the group at Learning Policy Institute, Zaretta Hammond, Stephanie Jones, Deborah Donahue-Keegan and her colleagues at the Massachusetts Consortium for Social-Emotional Learning in Teacher Education (SEL-TEd), Ann McKay Bryson, Debra Watkins, Marilyn Watson, Sandy Holman, and Learning Forward. The Fellows who have participated in our Teacher Educator Institutes have been an important source of feedback, support, and continuing motivation. Rochonda Nenonene, Rachel Collopy, and their colleagues at the University of Dayton, Elizabeth Brennan and Nancy Myers at California Lutheran University, and Kirk Kirkwood at CalState TEACH have helped us to gather data on this work and continue to expand our thinking. In addition, there are so many friends and colleagues who have taken precious time to talk with us, listen to and challenge our ideas, and share their own experiences as students, teachers, and faculty—we thank them all.

Above all, we are grateful to our families for their unflagging support of the book, our work, and us as people. In particular, Suzanne thanks her husband, Chris, who shows her every day what support and teamwork really mean, and her children, who are always generous with hugs and only occasionally asked, "Are you done with the book yet?" Nancy is grateful for the influence of her parents, Alice and Alex Lourié, who instilled in her, and modeled in their own work, the importance of paying attention to the whole person. She thanks her daughter Andie for cheering her mom on in this endeavor, always being open to sharing a window into the world of transracial adoption, and contributing many insights that informed this work. Finally, Nancy thanks her husband, Frank, who has been an unwavering champion of her work over the years and enthusiastically supported this book. He provided valuable insights and editorial assistance, as well as a sense of humor and collaborative spirit that helped keep us going.

About the Authors

NANCY LOURIÉ MARKOWITZ is the founder and executive director of the Center for Reaching & Teaching the Whole Child (CRTWC) and professor emerita in the Department of Teacher Education at San José State University. While at SJSU she taught courses including Creating an Effective Learning Environment and Social Studies Methods, as well workshops on effective coaching practices. She has also led major programmatic initiatives, including founding and directing both the Annenberg-funded university-district partnership, known as the Triple "L" Collaborative, and the award-winning SJSU Multiple Subject Teacher Education Collaborative Residency Program. She was selected as a Carnegie Foundation for the Advancement of Teaching Scholar, where she researched building professional learning communities among university teacher educators. Previously, she worked as an inner-city elementary school teacher in the Los Angeles Unified School District and as a K–8 private school administrator. Her most recent work includes the development, implementation, and evaluation of the Teacher Educator Institute, an innovative program to scale CRTWC's work of integrating the social, emotional, and cultural competencies in teacher preparation programs for teacher educators across the country. She is intent on drawing attention to the teacher professional development pipeline as a key lever of change. Her passion is to transform schools into places where both students and their teachers learn and thrive.

SUZANNE M. BOUFFARD is a researcher and writer with a PhD in psychology and a passion for making research useful and accessible. Her book, *The Most Important Year: Pre-Kindergarten and the Future of Our Children* (Avery, 2017), has been reviewed by national media including NPR and the *New York Times*. Her first book for Harvard Education Press, *Ready, Willing, and Able: A Developmental Approach to College Access and Success*, coauthored with Mandy Savitz-Romer, has been widely used by practitioners and policymakers around the country. She is currently the vice president of publications at Learning Forward and editor of *The Learning Professional* magazine. Prior to that, she spent ten years at the Harvard Graduate School of Education, where her research and writing focused on social and emotional learning (SEL), early childhood education, and family and community engagement in learning. She helped develop an SEL program called SECURe and helped launch the Making Caring Common initiative. Previously, with the Harvard Family Research Project, she led training and professional development for educators and conducted strategy development and program evaluation for nonprofits. Her writing has appeared in the *New York Times*, the *Atlantic*, the Daily Beast, *U.S. News and World Report*, and other national outlets, as well as education publications including *Harvard Education Letter, Educational Leadership, Social Policy Report*, and *Kappan*.

Index